AF241835

THE BOOK OF BRILLIANCE:

SELECTIONS FROM SEFER HA-BAHIR

ANNOTATED AND INTERPRETED

GEOFFREY W. DENNIS

Gutter Mystic Press

The Book of Brilliance
Copyright © 2026 Geoffrey W. Dennia

All Rights Reserved

ISBN: 978-1-967517-13-8

Without limiting the rights under copyright reserved above, no part of this publication may be reproduced, stored in or introduced into a retrieval system, or transmitted, in any form, or by any means (electronic, mechanical, photocopying, recording, or otherwise), without the prior written permission of both the copyright owner and the above publisher of this book.

Cover art: Abraham Lilien

*For my congregants, colleagues, and students
everywhere.
May they be blessed with all they need.*

CONTENTS

PREFACE

THE BOOK RESULTED from my teaching at the University of North Texas. I have been an adjunct instructor there in Jewish Studies since 1999 and began teaching my undergraduate Kabbalah course in 2006, coinciding with researching and writing my first book for Llewellyn, the *Encyclopedia of Jewish Myth, Magic, and Mysticism*. A key element of that course was to have students read Jewish mystical texts in translation in order to cultivate their ability to decipher, understand, and interpret [translated] primary sources.

To accomplish this, I have used a variety of published works. But I immediately found myself struggling to offer my students a useful translation of what I considered the most foundational of kabbalistic texts, *Sefer ha-Bahir*.

It was not the case that I had no options in English, a problem with many other works in the Jewish mystical tradition, rather that the existing options were all unsatisfactory in one fashion or another. Excluding excerpted translations that appear in academic articles and books, there are three choices for the English reader that existed before I wrote this book: an almost complete English version by the noted translator Joachim Neugroschel, which appeared in the anthology *the Secret Garden* (1976, David Meltzer, ed.); a complete translation with commentary by a famed rabbi, Aryeh Kaplan, entitled simply, *the Bahir* (1979); and a short selection of translations by the veteran Israeli scholar Joseph Dan that were included in his own anthology, *Early Jewish Mysticism* (1985). Each is worth knowing, yet each, in its own way, proved inadequate for my work introducing the English-language reader in Kabbalah to this seminal work.

In the case of Neugroschel, his translation is too minimalist, for it stands alone, unadorned by explanation. It lacks any sort of annotation, commentary, or useful introduction to help the reader make sense of the often obscure and baffling rhetoric of the *Bahir*. And then there is the other problem, that the book that contains it is out of print.

Rabbi Kaplan's book, by contrast, has remained in print since its first publication. Moreover, it includes a very elaborate commentary. Sadly, his apparatus, based largely on other, premodern Jewish kabbalistic commentaries, obscures as much as it reveals and often misleads the reader as to what the *Bahir* meant in its original context. This is not the result of poor scholarship, per se, but of faulty premises. For Kaplan approaches the text in an entirely a-historical fashion. The traditional interpreters anachronistically retrojected their later kabbalistic doctrines onto the *Bahir,* and Kaplan replicates this error. Two problems arise from this. First, Kaplan imposes on the text a very elaborate and ramified model of the *Sefirot,* a model that only developed centuries after the *Bahir*'s contributors lived. This distorts the *Bahir*, imposing meanings that are forced *upon* the text (eisegesis) rather than derived *from* the text (exegesis). Worse, for the general reader, Kaplan's commentary often consists of merely trying to assign a particular *sefirah* to each of the figures and symbols appearing in the *Bahir*, at times reducing his explanation to what is basically a *Sefirotic* game of Clue ("It is Yesod, using Malchut, in Beriyah"). Suffice to say that rather than elucidating, Rabbi Kaplan too often added an additional layer of obscurity.

As for Dr. Dan's translations and explanatory notes, I find them entirely clear, if too concise. No, the problem with his selection is that it is simply too small. A mere ten sections, all focused on the issue of *Sefirot,* simply does not give the English reader a real taste of the breadth and richness of the *Bahir* literature.

But it is from his exemplary approach that this project found its model. Following his lead, I created for my students an additional ten sections with annotations, which I used to supplement his work. As I found I wanted to emphasize other key concepts of the Kabbalah, I added occasional additional translations.

And so things stood, until I started working on the revised, expanded second edition of my *Encyclopedia of Jewish Myth, Magic, and Mysticism* in 2014. While working together on this, the wonderful acquisitions editor at Llewellyn, Elysia Gallo, asked me the question: "Do have any other books you would like to propose?" At first, my answer was "no." Then, thinking about my little bundle of annotated translations, I responded, "Well . . . I have something, but I don't think Llewellyn would find it interesting." At her urging, I sent her my selections, along with an introduction and a formal proposal for what you see, and to my delight, this adventuresome publisher agreed.

In finishing this book, I want to thank my Colleague-readers, who offered many material improvements to this work: Rabbi George Gittelman, Rabbi Max Weiss, Rabbi Ben Sternman, Rabbi Charlie Cytron-Walker, and Rev. James Hader. Most of all, I want to acknowledge the light of my eyes and the lamp for my feet, my love, my wife, Robin Paglia-Dennis.

And so, dear reader, here it is, my selection of fifty teachings from *Sefer ha-Bahir.* I hope you will find that I have avoided the pitfalls of earlier efforts, and that this edition will give you a fuller appreciation for this remarkable and mysterious work.

Geoffrey W. Dennis,
At the waxing crescent moon, Sh'vat, 5, 5776/Jan. 15, 2016.

PREFACE TO THE GUTTER MYSTIC BOOKS REPRINT

I DON'T NORMALLY see myself as a prophet, but in the case of *Sefer ha-Bahir*, I nailed it when I predicted its sales would not rise to the heights of my phenomenally successful *Encyclopedia of Jewish Myth, Magic, and Mysticism*. Not that it sold badly, but the publisher informed me there was no need for a second printing. And I still am flattered that a used copy now sells on Amazon for $248.00.

Still, I was sad to see it go out of print. The hardcover first edition was truly beautiful, and I'm still teaching my university class on Kabbalah. I sorely wished I could keep it on the syllabus as a recommended book (but not at $248.00 a copy). In 2020, I reclaimed rights to it. It sat on my computer until 2024, when a conversation with John Baltisberger, fellow Jew, fellow Texan, and prolific writer/publisher, rekindled the possibility of it returning to print. I proposed, and he proposed to include a new version of *The Book of Brilliance* under his Gutter Mystic Books imprint.

And now, here it is, at last, in a truly affordable format. I am grateful for John's enthusiasm (he was sending me cover designs within a week of my proposal). But I also am appreciative of my editor, Lisa Lee Tone, who meticulously combed over the PDF and found multiple opportunities for me to clarify my thoughts and correct some of my worst grammatical and syntactical tics. She is truly a great editor and collaborating with her was a genuine pleasure.

So it is with great pleasure to once again offer *Sefer ha-Bahir: Selections from the Book of Brilliance* to the reading public. Thanks to you for taking an interest. I hope you find it as rewarding to read as it was for me to write.

On the full moon, 14th of Sivan 5785
Geoffrey W. Dennis

INTRODUCTION

TO READ *Sefer ha-Bahir*, "The Book of Brilliance," is to discover where Kabbalah began. Gershom Scholem, the dean of modern Jewish mystical studies, has said that the *Bahir* is " . . . assuredly one of the most astonishing, not to say incredible, books in the Hebrew literature of the Middle Ages."[1] In ways unlike any Hebrew text before it, it brims with innovative imagery, opaque language, and what Daniel Abrams calls a "hermeneutic self-confidence."[2] It set a new standard for mystical rhetoric and speculation. There are more-well-known works of Kabbalah—the *Zohar*, the teachings of Isaac Luria, Hasidic literature—but all these emanate, at least in part, from this radiant book.

Written largely in the form of a commentary on Scripture, it is not an easy text to decode. The obscurity of the writing is not accidental; it is programmatic. More often than an explanation, each text is meant as a puzzle. Clarity is the exception rather than the rule. The reader has to earn the insights it offers, which may be part of its genius in captivating centuries of readers. While it frequently starts from Scripture and returns to Scripture, the *Bahir* understands the Hebrew Bible (*TaNaKH,* in Hebrew) in a remarkably different way than other interpreters of Holy Writ, both before and after it. Most people engage the Bible for what we believe it teaches us about ourselves, for we assume, as Abraham Joshua Heschel has said, that "The Bible is God's anthropology."[3] The *Bahir*, by contrast, treats the Hebrew Bible as God's physiology. It assumes Hebrew Scriptures to be a cryptic confession of God's inner nature, as well as a key to unlocking the invisible workings that unfold between the endless and ineffable God and our finite and material world. To convey these impossible revelations, *Sefer ha-Bahir* is, at turns, wildly imaginative, enigmatic, playful, contradictory, exasperating in its language, and shocking in its insights. It employs a kaleidoscopic, ever-shifting symbolic vocabulary to express a varied but compact set of ideas, which it presents not as a linear set of propositions but as a rich fabric of interwoven associations, each one simultaneously overlapping and underlying the diverse yet connected notions around it.

Who Wrote the *Bahir*?

We don't really know. Earlier generations were quite confident about its authorship. For centuries, it was assumed to have been written by the 1st Century Mishnaic Sage Rabbi Nehunya ben ha-Qanah-, who is mentioned on the first page of the book. Rabbi Nehunya seemed a logical choice, as he was a rabbi who figured prominently in the mystical *Hechalot* ("divine palaces") literature of antiquity. The appearance in the book of other sages from the same period adds to the sense that this is a document from antiquity.

Yet as intuitively logical as this all is, there is no literary reference in other sources to any part of *Sefer ha-Bahir,* or its alternate name, *Midrash Rabi Nehunya ben ha-Qanah-*, prior to the 12th Century. So rather than accept the traditionalist belief that it was kept a complete secret for over a thousand years, and noting that it includes linguistic and intellectual elements that are clearly medieval, modern academics conclude it was composed closer to that latter period. Some have argued that the most likely author was the well-known esoteric master of medieval Provence, Isaac the Blind. More recently, other academics have cast serious doubts on that claim. They argue that it is more likely there is no single author, that the *Bahir* was, for several centuries, an "open book," a compilation of several sources and rewrites ("strata") stretching from the 10th to 13th centuries, composed in places as far removed from each other as Iraq and Southern France. In short, *Sefer ha-Bahir* is a kind of mystical Wikipedia, the collective result of several unknown authors, and probably editors as well.[4]

How is *Bahir* Organized?

There are those who would say it isn't. One observer has written that it looks like it was put together after the pages were scattered by the wind. The modern textual scholar Reuven Margolioth published a version of it based on manuscript and early printed editions that he divided into 200 numbered sections. The greatest 20th century researcher of Kabbalah, Gershom Scholem, produced another version separated into 150 sections. Most recently, the scholar Daniel Abrams has produced a critical edition of the Hebrew text based on Scholem's arrangement. But regardless, it seems at times all the current arrangements of the sections defy sense; several long homilies are out of order, while in other cases, passages that seem like they might belong together are far removed from each other. Still, there is a rough logic to the homilies. Some passages are mostly devoted to explaining the metaphysics of the Creation. We also find a cluster of homilies explaining the mystical significance of the Hebrew Alphabet. This is followed by interpretations of the *Sefirot*, the divine emanations believed to be the organizing principles of Creation, and finally, more sections are devoted to the nature of the human soul and the doctrine of reincarnation. That being said, almost all the topics overlap each other, appearing and reappearing unpredictably in all parts of the book. To provide clarity for the modern reader, I have organized the passages collected here topically.

The Style of the *Bahir*

The *Bahir* is loosely constructed around the frame of a teacher and his disciples in debate. As with earlier rabbinic literature, it is unlikely that these are transcripts of actual conversations but a method of placing ideas in the form of a dialogue. This is somewhat analogous to Plato's use of his teacher Socrates as a figure to convey Plato's ideas. Within that framework, the most common stylistic elements include midrash, wordplay, the extensive use of parables, and elaborate mythic imagery.

Midrash is a uniquely Jewish form of Bible commentary that usually focuses on a single verse, or even a single word. Once the author establishes the interpretation to be drawn from the base or source text, then other verses (proof-texts) are brought in to reinforce, reshape, or expand the interpretation. One of the challenges for the English reader of Midrash is the interpretation often hinges on a quirk of Biblical Hebrew: a peculiar word order, an oddity of spelling or grammar, or the ambiguous meaning of a phrase. These anomalies are understood to be intentional; they are clues left for us by the divine mind. Of course, most of these features disappear in translation. This book will attempt to make the logic of these "close readings" in the original Hebrew as clear as possible.

Another barrier is the *Bahir* will often only cite a small part of the relevant biblical passage, assuming the readers know the Bible well enough to make all the connections without having all the information on the page in front of him or her. In this volume, I will include the extended context of a verse in the notes to help the reader appreciate the full impact of the interpretation. At times, the *Bahir* doesn't even mention a verse that seems to be informing the discourse. In such cases, I will present such a verse on the same page with the *Bahir* text.

Closely related to the midrashic technique, **wordplay** is a key interpretive tool of the *Bahir*. The use of wordplay was already commonplace in Midrash, but the *Bahir* pushes this to its limits. Probably the most prominent form of this is the use of *polysemy*. Polysemy refers to the fact that a word can have multiple, diverse, and even contradictory (think of the English word "cleave," which can mean either to *cut apart* or *cling together*) meanings. The *Bahir* often rejects a more commonly accepted meaning for a Hebrew word found in the Bible in favor of a less common but still plausible meaning, one that makes a given verse better serve as a proof-text for one of the *Bahir*'s core teachings. One can also find *notarikon,* the dividing of a single word, or combining of adjoining words, to yield a different reading. There is also the technique of *Al tikra,* "Don't read it as . . . but as . . . ." (Think of how just changing the accent point of the English word "convict" can shift it from a noun to a verb). All these techniques of variant reading find validity in the fact that, in its original form, the Hebrew Bible had neither vowels, punctuation, nor a standardized method of spelling words such as a dictionary. In these texts, it is not clear where verses, or even words, begin and end. The same word can be spelled differently just a few verses apart. Conveying all this in translation is very difficult, and I have striven to make these wordplays as clear as possible. Nevertheless, the reader who references some of the translations appearing in this book against one of the standard English Bible translations (which rarely agree in the exact wording themselves) will see, at times, startling differences. Such translations are not accidents or (I hope) simply poor scholarship but an effort to reveal what the contributors to the *Bahir* were attracted to in the wording.

Parable is a very old form of rhetoric that uses a simple, rather streamlined story, usually involving a few figures (a king, a princess, and a wedding contract, for example). The story is "parabolic," meaning it's not really about a king, a princess, and a contract; rather, the story serves as a simple allegory for more important ideas or relationships, usually God, the Jewish people, and the Torah. The *Bahir* has a particularly rich concentration of parables.

Like fairy tales ("Once upon a time . . . "), Jewish parables follow certain conventions. At the risk of oversimplification, there are usually three parts to a Jewish parable. Once the central concept or teaching has been established in a homily, there will be an introductory line, either "To what can this be compared?" or simply "A parable." The parable itself (called a *mashal* in Hebrew) will follow. In most cases, it will end with a *nimshal*, a statement that makes explicit the meaning of the parable. As we will see, the *Bahir* occasionally tinkers with these conventions, though it usually stays true to the model. More importantly, be prepared that the parables here will take the reader to strange places. These parables have figures that, for example, unexpectedly change gender. Sometimes, the parables present the reader with odd, even scandalous analogies about God and the world that may trouble us, or even offend us. Keep always in mind *Bahir* is trying to convey supernal forces and relationships that defy full and adequate explanation.

Mythic imagery is the use of iconic symbolic objects and figures from the Bible and rabbinic literature, usually involving divine or supernal entities: angels, the watery abyss, God's chariot, a tree, a throne, or a crown.

Judaism teaches there is one God, but that does not mean that Jewish ideas about God are simple. Jewish mysticism, especially, works from a manifold inheritance of Scripture, Jewish tradition, neo-Platonism, and Gnosticism, and sees a complex array of attributes, forces, qualities, and entities, such as angels, who "participate" in the divinity of the God of Israel, even as God in essence is ineffable and impossible to describe or define. Modern scholars will refer to this divine structure around and in God as the *Pleroma*, from the Greek "I fill" or "[divine] fullness." It is also characterized as the "Godhead." Sometimes, the Bible and rabbinic literature envision God's *Pleroma* as a royal entourage, "the heavenly court." A related mythic expression of the Godhead found in rabbinic literature is the Seven *Hechalot*, seven divine "Palaces" and their angelic denizens that make up the heavenly order.

Among the most compelling and recurrent Jewish image of the Godhead is taken from the vision of God on his Chariot-Throne that appears in Chapter 1 of the Book of Ezekiel. In this vision, God is surrounded by supernal colors, lights, celestial beasts, and sentient wheels. All these images are understood to convey secrets about how Divinity is structured and how God interacts with the world. In particular, mythic symbols are meant to show that the forces and entities Above and Below parallel each other and participate in a continuum of being. Thus, in Jewish mystical parlance, the *Pleroma* of the God of Israel comes to be referred to as the *Merkavah*, the "Chariot."

At its most revolutionary, the *Bahir* is subsuming all these earlier ideas into a new "unified field" version of the *Pleroma*, the *Sefirot*. The *Bahir* draws on the existing connotations its readers will associate with these mythic things (i.e., "throne" signifies power and dominion, or thinking of "ten" as a number that simultaneously signifies human and divine features) but also develops them in new and sometimes surprising ways. Often in the *Bahir*, these images become rather fluid metaphors with multiple mystical meanings. In many cases, they become encoded emblems for the divine powers that link God to the world. This brings us to the principle ideas and themes of the *Bahir*: The masculine and feminine aspects of deity, and the Sefirot.

Kabbalah scholar Moshe Idel dubs this mystical belief one God with a bi-sexual nature "di-theism."[5] It becomes, along with the *Sefirot*, one of the distinctive and enduring features of kabbalistic thought. But the *Bahir* goes beyond positing that there is a feminine dimension to God. It teaches that God bequeathed this divine attribute to everything. Every important aspect of reality, according to the *Bahir*, is made up of male and female counterparts. Drawing on the pronounced tendency of the Bible to talking in terms of *merisms* (polar ideas that encompass a greater whole) like "heaven and Earth," "light and dark," "great and small," "good and evil," "first and last," the author(s) of *Bahir* sees male and female polarities in the different forms and manifestations of commonplace and human phenomena like water, plants, letters, and even ritual acts.

And Now for Something Completely Different

One of the most striking features of the *Bahir* is, in fact, an absence, a surprising de-emphasis of something that is quite prominent in later kabbalistic writings—moral dualism. The idea of a radical dichotomy between good and evil is largely reconceptualized here as a dialectic process. And the themes of good and evil are almost entirely encapsulated in four (11, 161, 162, 200) of the 200 sections of the Margolioth edition. There are, without question, many dualisms to be found in this work: male and female, East and West, Justice and Compassion, strength and weakness, right and left. But while we meet angels and other denizens of heaven, the *Bahir* has only the faintest interest in demons. Satan does appear, not as God's nemesis but as God's servant and prosecuting attorney. The *Bahir* certainly does refer to evil but never as an ontological force apart and distinct from the divine *Pleroma* and divine purpose. It is also plainly concerned with its readers cultivating righteous behaviors because such behaviors strengthen God's presence and power. Yet moral condemnation and reproof is simply not a preeminent feature of the book, something many modern readers may find refreshing.

How this Book is Organized

Because of all the complexities described above, this collection has grouped the translated selections topically rather than in the sequence as it appears in the *Bahir*, although the number of the homily in the Hebrew text will appear at the top of the page as XX (M) for the Margolioth text, and as XX (S-A) for the Scholem-Abrams text. Occasionally, the reader will see only one citation. This is because not every teaching appears in both the base manuscripts used by these scholars. A table at the back of the book will allow you to quickly locate a passage by matching this number to the page number where it appears. Drawing from both the Margolioth and Scholem-Abrams texts, for this collection, I have selected fifty of the most piquant and accessible passages, enough to allow the reader to see the full scope of the *Bahir*'s interests but sparing the reader both the plainly fragmented sections and the often repetitive nature of the complete work, which revisits the same concise cluster to themes multiple times. Some translations will be the complete rendering of the section, some will span more than one, while others will be a shorter excerpt chosen because it reflects a single mystical concept or insight.

All passages will begin with a title of my own devising. Most passages will end with a biblical or, in a few cases, a rabbinic passage that helped inspire or at least relates to the homily. These are included in this edition because oftentimes such passages are not cited completely, or even at all, in the Hebrew original. These verses will be rendered in italics to alert the reader that they are not part of the original *Bahir* text. Explanatory notes will appear on the left-hand page of the open book, facing the translation. One can read the section to its end, as one would read a poem, and only then consult the annotations on the facing page. But the *Bahir* was probably meant to be studied rather than merely read, so it may be more fruitful for someone not conversant with Jewish and mystical rhetoric to consult the notes each time a superscription is reached. If, along the way, you forget the meaning of specific concepts, like *Sefirot* or *merkavah,* a glossary of Hebrew and Aramaic terms will be included at the end of the book you can earmark.

A Note on Translation

In modern translations of Hebrew texts, it has become conventional to avoid the use of the gender-based pronoun "he" in reference to God, usually by substituting "God" for "He," in order to honor the conventional Jewish theology that God is beyond gender. However, the kabbalistic notion of divinity as bi-gendered is so central to *Sefer ha-Bahir,* I have opted to eschew that contemporary convention and allow the issue of masculine and feminine references to divinity be in the foreground of this translation. I hope the reader will indulge me in this approach.

Some Last Thoughts

Like the locations and time periods of the *Bahir*'s composition, modern scholars have tried to trace the ideas and movements that have had an influence on its composition. Beyond the internal traditions of Judaism, so obvious, various scholars make good arguments for the presence of Pagan, Hellenistic philosophical, Gnostic, and even early Judeo-Christian ideas underlying various teachings.[6] If we take all this to be true—that *Sefer ha-Bahir* is a work of centuries, composed on different continents, all along the way incorporating a variety of interpretations and perspectives—then we need to recognize this archly Jewish book is also a work of unusual pluralism, a remarkably eclectic body of teachings with roots in many communities. I happen to think that makes *Sefer ha-Bahir* a book uniquely suited for our age. I hope you find this strange and beautiful work as intriguing, rewarding, and inspiring as I do.

GEOFFREY W. DENNIS

TABLE OF ARRANGEMENT IN THE RECEIVED TEXT
(MARGOLIOTH; SCHOLEM-ABRAMS)

In the Beginning: The Mystical Quest

PERHAPS THE BIGGEST challenge to the study of mysticism is defining the word itself. What constitutes a mystical idea, text, experience, or practice? Pinning down what precisely we are talking about when we label something "mystical" has proven quite elusive. There are some modern scholars who even argue that mysticism is in fact a meaningless term, a made-up category of phenomenology invented by academics looking in on religious and ritual practices they otherwise do not know how to characterize. When an outsider looks at the practice of Episcopalians, who sing decorously from their pews, compared to, say, the practice of Charismatics, who dance, shout, shake, roll their eyes, and speak in tongues, it is hard to see them as both belonging the same religious phenomenon called Christianity. So the term "mystical" gets applied to one but not the other. Yet for someone inside Christianity, that distinction may not be meaningful. The Charismatic experience may be regarded merely a more intense shade, a different tone of piety, as it were, but not different in essence when seen on the broad color spectrum of Christian devotional practices.

Yet others persist in the claim that mysticism is a thing unto itself. Not only a radically different kind of religion but not necessarily religion at all. Cannot a totally a-religious scientist, for example, have deeply mystical thoughts about nature, or feel a transrational exhilaration about the universe that is more than merely understanding the sum of the knowledge being considered?

So various definitions have been proposed:

The desire to achieve complete union with God, or the Absolute.

Related to the first: pursuing a transcendent object of desire with totality of purpose. This pursuit is usually characterized as driven by "love" but often takes on erotic overtones, i.e., "erotic theology," in which the intimacy enjoyed between human lovers is the paradigmatic experience sought.

The apprehension of knowledge or reality beyond what may be attained by intellectual study alone; often, intuition, sudden insight, epiphany, or revelation that serves to supplement what can be known through reason.

Esoteric, occult, or secret beliefs and doctrines not to be known or to be shared with the general public or the broader community.

As it turns out, what we generally characterize as "Jewish mysticism" has encompassed, at different times and different places, all these elements. Though people today simply refer to Jewish mysticism as "Kabbalah," there have been many and diverse esoteric and pietistic traditions which have appeared within Judaism, and many of them, such as Merkavah mysticism and German Pietism, predate the appearance of the kabbalistic tradition, which has been widely regarded as being initiated by *Sefer ha-Bahir*. And novel as it is, a major feature of the *Bahir* is how it adapts and assimilates these earlier systems, striving towards a new synthesis of metaphysics, rhetoric, and experience.

Honestly, I could try to describe Jewish mysticism in all its range and complexity, but my explanation would pale against the incomparable essay written over a half-century ago by the theologian Abraham Joshua Heschel, "The Mystical Element in Judaism" (reprinted, also with others of his many seminal articles, in the 1997 *Moral*

Grandeur and Spiritual Audacity). Let it suffice us to consider just one quote from that great article: "[Jewish mystics] want to taste the whole grain of the spirit before it is ground by the millstones of reason."

This particular aspect of Jewish mysticism, the mystical quest, constitutes the first of the topical materials brought together in this book. What follows in this first section are four teachings about the desire and goals of the one who seeks to pierce the veil of this world, see beyond mere appearances, and experience the truth that he (or she) believes underpins reality.

There are four sections included here. The first addresses how the paradox of the mystical quest is not paradox at all, from God's perspective, and therefore not futile; the second, the human daring entailed in the mystical quest; the third, its thrilling and enthralling dimension; the final passage assures the seeker that failure is not only inevitable but a necessary part of the quest.

Texts elsewhere in this collection which have content related to this section: §70(M); §48(S-A); §72(M); §49 (S-A)

PIERCING THE PARADOX
§1(M); §1 (S-A)

Rabbi Nechunya ben haKanah taught: It is written in one verse, stating,

Now, one cannot see light, though it is brilliant in the heavens . . . (Job. 37:21).1
But in another one it states, **He made darkness his cover** . . . (Ps. 18:12).2
[And elsewhere it states, **Dense clouds surround Him** (Ps. 97:2)].3
This is a contradiction, yet a third verse comes and harmonizes them,4
For it states, **Even the darkness is not too dark for You,**
night shines like day; darkness and light are the **same** (Ps. 139:12).5

RELATED BIBLICAL VERSE:

Now, one cannot see light, though it is brilliant in the heavens, until the spirit passes and cleanses them (Job. 37:21).

1. . . . though it is brilliant in the heavens. The word *Bahir* ("brilliance") gives this work its title. Like so many mystical works, *Sefer ha-Bahir* begins with a paradox—light that cannot be perceived. For the purposes of the teaching, the light is understood to refer to God. In the Talmud's earlier use of this same verse, this brilliance is the light of divine instruction (T. B. *Ta'anit* 7b).

2. He made darkness his cover. Mythically, darkness is the antipode of light, the inert condition that reigned before the spirit of God enlightened the cosmos (Gen. 1:2-4). How, then, can the dark also be a divine thing? The paradox deepens.

3. Dense clouds surround Him. This buttresses the second verse, that the true nature of divinity is concealed from us. This verse is bracketed for reasons explained in the next note.

4. Yet a third verse comes. The keen observer notices that Ps. 139 is in fact the fourth verse cited. Since Ps. 97:2 is missing from some manuscripts, it is likely that a later editorial hand added it because 97:2 seemed thematically relevant, though it otherwise interrupts the elegant poetics (thesis-antithesis-synthesis) of the teaching.

5. Darkness and light are the same. Ultimately, all paradoxes are resolved in the One, all contradictions reconciled. But what of us? Must we remain prisoners to the apparent incoherence of the world? The answer to that, though left unstated in the teaching, is nonetheless to be found in the unrecorded continuation of the of each of the first two verses: . . . *until the spirit passes and cleanses them* (Job 37:21) and . . . *Out of the radiance of His clouds blazing hail passed over* (Ps. 18:13). This deliberate ellipsis introduces another feature of mystical texts: occultism. The author assumes the unworthy will read what is quoted

and look no further. The potential initiate, by contrast, will either know or find what follows and the message they convey: those who are seekers of wisdom will, in time, be purified and initiated into the mysteries of the All, the gloom pierced and concealed light will be unveiled for them, revealing nuggets of enlightenment. This quest to penetrate the darkness that shrouds the visible world is the subject of *Sefer ha-Bahir*.

GEOFFREY W. DENNIS

THE PARABLE OF
THE CONCEALED KING
§71(M); §49(S-A)

Thus [the prophet] Habakkuk said, "I know my
prayer was received with delight,
So I was delighted when it brought me to that
unnamed place.1
And **I understood Your thought, and I am afraid**
. . . (Hab. 3:2).2
Therefore, . . . **YHVH, enliven Your works in the
midst of years** (Hab. 3:2).
In Your unity."3
A parable. What does this resemble?
A guarded, miraculous, and concealed king,
who entered his palace and ordered [his subjects],
do not petition him.4
Therefore any who seek him are afraid lest the
king know that he transgressed his command.5
Thus one says [first], "I am afraid. **YHVH, enliven
Your works in the midst of years."**6
So says Habakkuk, "Since Your name is like You
are,
therefore Your works will forever
enliven Your name in the midst of years."7

RELATED BIBLICAL TEXT:

*It is the glory of God to conceal a matter; to
search out a matter is the glory of kings (Job
25:2).*

1. **That unnamed place.** Other than the idea that the prophet engaged in mystical contemplation and achieved some higher knowledge of God, we cannot be sure what this refers to. Perhaps he achieved a vision of the divine *merkavah,* had a mystical ascent through the seven heavens, or ascended the rungs of the *Sefirot.* Whatever it was, he achieved a state of ecstasy in proximity to God.

2. **And I am afraid.** The intimate encounter with the ultimate is always a mix of joy and terror, of awe and awfulness (Is. 6:1-6), of blessing and dread (Gen. 32:1-10). The Hebrew word used here, *yarei,* simultaneously means "fear" and "awe."

3. **Enliven your acts . . . in unity.** Balance the forces of love and judgment in the world. Do not allow the material universe to sway too much to one divine attribute or another; balance Your Judgment with Your Mercy.

4. **Do not petition him.** Called a *mashal* in Hebrew, a parable is a streamlined figurative narrative that obliquely illustrates and illuminates a difficult or abstract concept. A common rhetorical and educational tool in rabbinic literature, here we meet the first parable in our arrangement. Up to this point, the teaching is obscure, so an analogy is offered to dealing with a mortal king. The king [God], disappointed and despairing of his subjects [the world], retreats from the thing he has created. The idea that the divine presence withdraws from the world when it turns wicked is an ancient Jewish trope (*Gen. R.* 19:7) and is variously referred to as God "hiding His face" (Deut. 32:20; Ezek. 39:29) or, in later Kabbalah, the "hidden light."

5. **He transgressed his command.** With all humility, the loyal subject refuses to take "no" for an answer from his king. The prophet-mystic will storm the closed gates of

heaven because the idea of the world devoid of blessing is unacceptable. This particular parable is an easy introduction to the genre; few other parables in the *Bahir* will prove so straightforward.

6. **Enliven Your works in the midst of years.** The continuation of the verse, . . . **though angry, you may remember compassion."** (Hab. 3:2), not included in the original text, provides the seeker reassurance that God, in fact, will respond. What is the content of the mystic's petition? It is not for personal benefit (the delight of being in God's presence is enough) but that God re-engage with the world and human history ("amidst the years").

7. **Your works will forever enliven Your name.** A convoluted sentence. I interpret this to mean that when the mystic stimulates God to engage with creation, the Divine presence ("Your name") will be seen by ordinary people and God's reputation will be enhanced. Reaching out to God draws God back into the world.

GEOFFREY W. DENNIS

GOD INTOXICATED
§68(M); §46(S-A)

The students of R. Rachumai asked him:
What [is the meaning of what] is written,
The prayer of Habakkuk the Prophet, concerning
  shigionot? (Hab. 3:1)1
A prayer? [He responded] It should be [read as]
  "praise."2
Rather, everyone who turns his heart from
  engagement with the [manifest] world
And contemplates the 'Workings of the Chariot,'3
Is received before the Blessed Holy One
As if he prayed the entire day.4
As it is written, **The prayer of Habbakuk.**5
And what [is the meaning of] **concerning**
  shigionot?
As it is written, **You will reel [*tishgeh*] in her love**
  constantly (Prov. 5:19).6
And what is . . . **her** . . . ? The Workings of the
  Chariot. 7

RELATED BIBLICAL TEXT:

You lay the beams of Your upper chambers on
their celestial waters. You make the clouds Your
chariot and ride on the wings of the wind (Ps.
104:3).

1. **The prayer of Habakkuk.** It is not clear if the students want an explanation of the whole verse or of the word *shigionot*. The teaching answers both. There is no confirmed meaning to the word itself, but most translators assume it is a music mode or style for the recital of the oracle, while others translate it as "erring ones."

2. **It should be "praise."** R. Rachumai reads it as "a praise of Habakkuk . . . concerning shigionot." How he arrives at this reading is not obvious. Perhaps it is because what follows in Chapter 3 is more akin to a paean to God than a prayerful petition or confession. Nevertheless, he is preparing the way to teach his students the value of mystical practice, which he will link back to the word "prayer."

3. **Workings of the Chariot.** *Ma'asei Merkavah* in Hebrew. This refers to the visions of the prophet Ezekiel in the 1st and 10th chapters of his book, in which he describes witnessing God's glorious chariot-throne and its attendant creatures in a vision of unsurpassed splendor and complexity. The term *merkavah* comes to stand for the *Pleroma*, the totality of the divine order, from the angels, emanations, attributes, and the structure of the seven heavens to God Himself, in so far as the limited human mind and soul can apprehend (also see Ps. 104:3; II Kings 2:11; Ps. 68:17). Investigating, contemplating, and/or even ascending through the *Merkavah* is a Jewish esoteric discipline that predates the *Bahir*. Some scholars use this passage as proof that the first versions of the *Bahir* were composed in Mesopotamia, where the speculation on the *Ma'asei Merkavah* originated.

4. **As if he prayed the entire day.** Engaging in esoteric disciplines should be regarded as an act of deepest piety, equal in value to the reciting of all the prayers mandated by Jewish tradition. This is a controversial claim. First, the

Talmud strongly cautions against engaging in esoteric pursuits, for they have great potential to harm the ill-prepared (*B. Chag.* 12b-14b); and second, this claim seems to flirt with anti-nomianism, suggesting mystical contemplation is a valid substitute for the authorized forms of Jewish worship. It is unlikely the writer is advocating the abandonment of Jewish practice, for elsewhere, the *Bahir* presents the common practices of Judaism as pregnant with powerful theurgic potential. Rather, he is reassuring the reader that his/her mystical quest is a valid and worthy pursuit.

5. **As it is written, The prayer of Habakkuk.** The reason the prophet chose to call it "prayer" was precisely to teach us that mystical investigation is equal to prayer.

6. **Concerning shigionot.** Now, the mysterious word is to be explained. The author believes the word is the same root as the imperfect verb *tishgeh,* "you will reel/you will be intoxicated."

7. **And what is . . . her . . . ?** The Proverbs verse uses the female pronoun. This refers to the *Merkavah*, which is a feminine noun. Seeking mystical encounter with the godhead is an intoxicating endeavor.

ERROR LEADS US TO ENLIGHTENMENT
§150(M); §100(S-A)

Rabbi Rachumai said,
Why is it written,
And a rebuke that instructs is the way of life
 (Prov. 6:23)?
Teaching that for all who study
The Workings of Creation and the Works of the
 Chariot,1
It is impossible not to stumble.2
But as it is written,
Take charge of this ruin! (Is. 3:6).
[Meaning] these are things that cannot be
 mastered,
except that one stumble in them.
So the Torah teaches, a rebuke that instructs . . .
But in truth, such makes one worthy [for]3
 . . . **the way** of life.4
Therefore, the one who desires to merit the way
 of life
Must [first] endure the rebuke that instructs.

RELATED BIBLICAL TEXT:

*For the commandments are a lamp, and the
Torah a light; And a rebuke that instructs is the
way of life* (Prov. 6:23).

1. The Workings of Creation and the Works of the Chariot. Mystical cosmogony and the nature of the Godhead, these are the subjects of *Sefer ha-Bahir.*

2. It is impossible not to stumble. This is much more nuanced than rabbinic warnings about pursing esoteric knowledge; the Sages indicate that error while engaged in occult pursuits leads straight to personal catastrophe (*B. Chag.* 14b).

3. **Such makes one worthy**. Mistakes and setbacks, endured and overcome, prepare one for learning the ultimate secrets attainable.

4. **The way of life.** The first half of the verse from Proverbs is not cited here, **For the commandment is a lamp, and the Torah is light . . . "The way of life,"** therefore, is enlightenment in the mysteries of **the cosmos,** which illuminate the ordinary teachings of Torah. The mystical quest is not a level path strewn with rose petals; it entails strife of the spirit, it risks psyche and ego. Yet it promises—All.

The Potency of the Hebrew Alphabet and Word Mysticism

B Y THE VERY fact that the Hebrew Bible reports God created the cosmos through speech-acts, Judaism has always regarded words, and particularly Hebrew words, as entities of power. As Eitan Fishbane writes, "The auto-emanation of the divine Being is thus the vocalization of a silent cosmic reality. God does not just speak the word of Creation. God *is* the word of Creation."[7] This belief in the constructive/divine power of words is highlighted by the oft-made observation that the Hebrew word *davar* simultaneously means "word" and "thing/entity/matter." This idea of language as a constructive force, as something that not only describes but participates in, even shapes our reality, anticipates some modern developments in philosophy and linguistics.

A theme *Sefer ha-Bahir* picks up from *Sefer Yetzirah*, as well as from magical beliefs from antiquity, is this idea that the Hebrew alphabet is not merely a set of phonetic symbols but a web of forces pregnant with spiritual potency. *Sefer ha-Bahir* goes so far as to regard the very shapes of the letters as full of divine intention, clues to how the letters function in building and sustaining the cosmos. The word of greatest importance, however, is God's own name, recorded here as the slightly inaccurate YHVH (though a *vav* in Modern Hebrew signifies a "v" sound, most scholars agree that in biblical Hebrew, a *vav* signified a "w" sound). This word stands at the very highest order of being and serves as the primordial scaffolding from which the cosmos is suspended.

Numbers, too, have their innate celestial power. As a practical matter, most ancient languages also used their alphabets as numbers. This is certainly true of Hebrew, in which *alef* has the value of 1, *bet* equals 2, and so on, shifting to multiples of 10 with the *kaf*, multiples of hundreds with *resh*, until the last letter, *tav*, equals 400. Since Jewish hermeneutics assume that the Scriptures are "all music and no noise," that there are no accidents in the meaning (or value) of words and letters, a "science" of numerology, called *Gematria,* developed, in which words are translated into their numeric value, and meaning, homiletic or mystical, is derived from that, often by finding another word with the same value.

Numbers that the *Bahir* finds particularly potent are three, seven, ten, and twelve. In some sections, older Jewish mystical traditions about seven—seven days, seven heavens, seven parts of the human body—prevail. In other parts, these merge with ten, both the *ma'amarot,* the ten divine utterances of Creation, and the organizing number of the *Sefirot.* Again and again, the *Bahir* emphasizes the movement from divine thought, to divine breath, and finally to divine sound; a transition from the concealed to the perceptible. The physical universe is, at its essence, God externalized through language.

The heading **Hebrew Alphabet and Word Mysticism** contains the largest collection of teaching included in this annotated selection. Still, it is far from comprehensive, encompassing the consonants *alef, bet, dalet, hay,* and the vowel *cholam.* Even in its complete text, the *Bahir* does not offer a systematic treatment of all twenty-two letters and six vowels of the Hebrew phonetic alphabet. Certain letters—*alef, bet, gimel*—inspire multiple interpretations, while others are completely neglected. Yet other letters merit only a passing observation.

For our selections, *To hear is the Beginning* and *The Holiness of Name and Place* explore the cosmic significance of the *alef,* associating it with divine thought that precedes creation itself, human thought at its inception, and even linking it to heavenly and earthly structures, as well as linking it with the divine name. *The World was Created Through Blessing* and *A House Built of Secrets* probe the question of why the Written Torah begins with the second letter, *bet,* rather than the first letter, *alef.* The *Cornucopia of Good* analyzes the shape of the third letter, *gimel,* to discover a concealed truth about metaphysics. *The Sound of the Soul, a Healing Jewel* shifts attention to a vowel sound for what it teaches about the human soul. In *Hay is the Portal to the World to Come*, the letter *hay* is examined for what it teaches on the divine-human relationship.

Again, this is only a sample of the *Bahir*'s treatment of the Hebrew alphabet, but if this is a major interest, the reader will find still more teachings embedded in other topics explored in this book.

Texts elsewhere in this collection which have content related to this section: §27(M); §14 (S-A); §53(M); §34 (S-A); §54(M); §36(S-A); §79(M); §53 (S-A); §80-81(M); §54-55(S-A); §83(M); §56(S-A); §141(M); §96(S-A).

GEOFFREY W. DENNIS

TO HEAR IS THE BEGINNING
§70(M); §48(S-A)

And why did he [Habakkuk] say, [I heard Your
thought] **and I was afraid** (Hab. 3:2)?1
Because the ear resembles an *alef*.2
And the *alef* is the first of all letters.3
Not only this, but the *alef* is the cause for the
existence of all the letters.4
And the *alef* resembles the brain.5
As when you [merely] open your mouth, you
make *alef*,6
So too, the thought you think is without boundary
or end.
And from the *alef* goes forth all the letters.
Do you not see that it is their head?
And it is written, **YHVH is at their head** (Micah
2:13).7

RELATED BIBLICAL TEXT:

***For the ear tests words as the tongue tastes food
(Job 34:3).***

1. [I heard Your thought]. Here, the focus on the Habakkuk verse we met earlier is not on the fear but on the audition that the prophet "hears" God's word. It is not obvious why the most important part of the verse was not cited.

2. The ear resembles an *alef*. Its curving, complex shape is reminiscent of the outer ear. But this also signifies that the ear corresponds with a divine creative emanation (*sefirah*), just as other body parts do (§ 82/55), correlating cosmos and humanity into one conceptual field. Each letter is regarded to have powers, so the divine choice of letters, words, and phrases in the Scriptures is not merely choosing the best words to form declaratives, imperatives, and interrogatives, but the best expression of fundamental realities embedded in the things they describe. Exactly which *sefirah* is not made clear here. It could be *Keter*, which is related to thought; or by making a wordplay on *alef* using the Talmudic saying, *aluf binah,* "the chieftain of insight" (*B. Shab.* 104a), it could mean *Chochmah*, the *sefirah* that ontologically precedes *Binah*.

3. The *alef* is the first. It is the first letter in the *alef-bet,* it has the numeric value of "one," but it is also cosmologically the source and origin of all the other letters which, by being used in divine speech-acts (Gen. 1:3–1:27), form Creation; it has priority over all.

4. *Alef* is the cause for the existence of all the letters. Again, the meaning is two-fold. All the features of the other letters—stems, curves, and points—are present in the *alef*, written manuscript style. At the same time, on a cosmic level, all subsequent letters emanate from it, just as the cosmos emanate from the thoughts of God.

5. *Alef* resembles the brain. *Alef* is a silent consonant; it makes no sound without a vowel. It is like thought, which "opens" to new conceptions yet is effectively unbounded

by the constraints of language, logic, or physics. This is especially true when contemplating God. By the same token, it remains unrealized until it triggers action ("speech"). The *Alef* is therefore analogous to the highest of the divine emanations, *Keter*, which has no positive existence and is closer to the undefined "no-thingness" of the Unknowable God (*Ein Sof*) than to the more active, realized existence of the lower *Sefirot*, the ten divine potencies (§ 179/§122) sketchily outlined in an earlier occult work, *Sefer Yetzirah*, that flow from it.

6. **Open your mouth**. In the opening act of creation, the *Ruach Elohim*, the "breath of God," swept over the primordial abyss (Gen. 1:2), a kind of divine exhalation, or catching one's breath, before the first words are uttered. Thus *Keter* releases *Chochmah*, "wisdom," the second *sefirah*. An earlier mystical text, *Sefer Yetzirah,* has already declared Wisdom the "breath of the living God" (1:9). This movement from thought to breath to sound signals the rise of the ingenious kabbalistic interpretation that through the model of the *Ein Sof* emanating the *Sefirot,* the Kabbalist can simultaneously embrace the respectable apophatic theology (that one can say nothing descriptive about God, who is wholly beyond any comparisons or analogies) so beloved of rationalist philosophy, and the catophatic (one can describe and relate to God in familiar terms like "loving," "just," and "compassionate") so craved by the religious believer.

7. **YHVH is at their head.** Having equated the *alef* with the mind of God and the soundless spirit that precedes speech, the most potent name of God is added to this cluster of concepts. While this last line seems to come out of nowhere, it's actually a bit of witty biblical exegesis—just as the ear is attached to the head, the *alef* is attached to God's great name. This, then, is the potency of the *alef*; it embodies the first and highest—of the senses, of the organs, of the divine names, and the creative process.

GEOFFREY W. DENNIS

THE HOLINESS OF NAME AND PLACE
§70(M); §48 (S-A)

And it has been established for us
Of every divine name that is written,
yud-hay-vav-hay is unique for the Holy One of
  blessing.1
And [it is] sanctified in holiness.2
And what is "in holiness?"
In the holy palace.3
And where is the "holy palace?"
In thought, which is *alef*,4
Which is why,
I heard Your thought and I was afraid (Hab. 3:2).

RELATED BIBLICAL TEXT:

YHVH is at their head (Micah 2:13).

1. *Yud-hay-vav-hay* Is unique. This teaching is a continuation of the previous teaching. The Hebrew Bible contains several different names and many different titles and monikers for God. The *Bahir* declares the Tetragrammaton, God's four-letter name is the most holy, confirming a belief held by the Talmudic Sages. The question to be addressed here is: how does this relate to the *Bahir*'s other teachings regarding the priority of divine emanations?

2. Sanctified in holiness. "Holiness" is the quality that links the divine name with what follows.

3. The holy palace. The most obvious meaning for this is the Temple in Jerusalem. In *Gen. R.* 1.4, the Temple is one of the six entities God conceptualized prior to beginning the creation. The Temple is therefore a very early high-stage in the process of divine emanation. In this case, it seems to be the first divine thought/emanation.

4. In thought, which is *alef*. A "chain midrash," a teaching that strings together verses constructed on the premise that "A=B=C=D=A," or, if one prefers, a syllogistic Ouroboros. The equation of holiness and God's name is made in the Bible (Pss. 103:1; 105:3). The correspondence of holiness with the Temple, *alef,* and thought is made in §§ 79, 117, and 153. Thus, through their shared association with "holiness," YHVH=thought=*alef.* This teaching is meant to resolve a set of potential contradictions, for in *Bahir* §17, *alef* is declared "at the head" (first emanation), but in the Bible, the Prophet Micah writes, "YHVH is at the head" (2:13). By making all of these elements conceptually synonymous, any potential contradiction is harmonized, bringing together the diverse threads of earlier metaphysical teachings and incorporating them in the model of the divine *Sefirot*. At the same time, the ambiguity and multiplicity of terms signals the ambiguity

of trying to describe God at the highest level. As much as we desire God be fully disclosed to us, all human analogies are inadequate in one way or another. The world offers us only flashes of insight to illumine our darkened path.

THE WORLD WAS CREATED THROUGH BLESSING
§3(M); §3 (S-A)

And why does [the Torah] begin with [the letter] *bet*?1

In order to begin with a blessing.2

And how do we know the Torah is called a blessing?

As it is written, **full of the blessing of YHVH is the sea,**

And the south he will possess (Deut. 33:23).3

And 'sea' only means 'Torah,' as it is written, **its measure is wider than the sea** (Job 11:10).4

And what does . . . **full of the blessing of YHVH** . . . mean?

Only that every place that *bet* is written, it is the expression of blessing.

As it is written, *Bereshit.* 5

There is no beginning without wisdom.6

As it is written, **The beginning of wisdom is the awe of YHVH** (Ps. 11:20).7

And there is no wisdom without blessing, as was written, **And God blessed Solomon** (I Kings 2:45),8

And it is written, **And YHVH granted wisdom to Solomon** (I Kings 5:26).

[this is comparable to] a parable of a king who marries his daughter to his son.

He gives her to him at the wedding and says to him, "Do with her as you desire."9

1. And why begin with *bet*? *Bet* is the second letter of the Hebrew alphabet and has the numerical value of 2. The Sages had asked centuries earlier, why should the first word in all the Torah—*Bereshit*, "at/when beginning"—not begin with the first letter, *Alef* (*S. of S. R.* 5:11)? A question made compelling by the mystical belief that the Hebrew letters are not merely phonetic symbols but cosmic potencies.

2. In order to begin with a blessing. The Hebrew word for blessing, *b'rachah*, like *bereshit* ("At the beginning"), starts with *bet*. This is assumed to be a meaningful convergence, not a mere coincidence. What follows is another chain midrash. Thus, Beginning=blessing=sea=Torah=wisdom=beginning.

3. Full of the blessing of YHVH is the sea, the south he will possess. We see here the *Bahir*'s hermeneutic of identifying common words in Scripture as bearers of esoteric meaning. In this case, "sea," which in context probably means "west," is understood by the commentator to mean "Torah." The linking of sea and Torah predates the *Bahir* (*B. Ber.* 61b; *B.K. 82a*). More puzzling is the interpretation of the word "south." The term has no special meaning to the Talmudic rabbis. In later kabbalistic writings, the south signifies Abraham and, by association, love, but that is not evident here. However, Deut. 33:23 is cited in other places in the *Bahir*, where it becomes clear that "south" means "this world/universe." The esoteric meaning is thus: The Torah, the repository of God's blessings, is the instrument through which the world/universe is created [and therefore it, too, is full of blessings].

4. Its measure is wider than the sea. The context of the quote is: **Oh, how I wish that God would speak, that He would open his lips to you and disclose to**

RELATED BIBLICAL TEXT:

Oh, how I wish that God would speak, that He would open his lips to you and disclose to you the secrets of wisdom, for understanding is two-fold. (Job 11:5-6).

you the secrets of wisdom . . . its measure is wider than the sea (Job. 11: 3-10). So Sea=Torah=wisdom (*Pesikta da Rav Kahana* 12:20; *Mid. Teh.* 104:22).

5. **As it is written.** We are reminded of the first word of the Torah, *Bereshit.*

6. *Reshit* is the Hebrew word for "beginning."

7. **There is no beginning without wisdom.** Wisdom is the instrument of world-formation, so *bet,* blessing=sea=Torah=wisdom=beginning.

8. **And there is no wisdom without blessing.** The two citations about Solomon demonstrate that the content of God's blessing is wisdom. Since the first word of Torah is *b-reshit*, "*bet* is the beginning," we now reach the end of the chain/syllogism: *bet*=beginning=blessing=sea=Torah= wisdom=blessing=*bet*, which precedes the beginning of the universe. Blessing and wisdom are manifest in all creative beginnings.

9. **A parable of a king.** This is our first encounter with many of the *Bahir*'s many strange and subversive parables. The Jewish use of parable as a tool to illuminate difficult concepts goes back to the Hebrew Bible. Here, the parable seems more obscure than the teaching preceding it, but the essence is this: the king is God. The daughter is wisdom/Torah, and the son is creation/world. God has given us his precious daughter without preconditions, giving us the complete freedom to use or misuse it/her, a great and (hopefully) uneasy power.

A House Built of Secrets
§14(M); §11 (S-A)

Why is the [letter] *Bet* closed on every side,
 but open to what follows it?1
To teach you that it is the house of the cosmos,2
[thus] it is [the case] that,
"God is the place of the world, but the world is not
    His place."3
So don't read it as '*bet*,' but '*bayit*'4
As it is written,
A house is built with wisdom [and established by
    understanding] (Prov. 24:3).5

RELATED BIBLICAL TEXT:

**Unless YHVH builds the house, the builders labor
in vain. Unless YHVH watches over the city, the
guards stand watch in vain (Ps. 127:2).**

1. Why is the *Bet* closed on every side? Like all Hebrew letters, *bet,* in effect, is a divine emanation. How does its shape reflect its celestial nature? As a box with one side open (ב), it contains all of creation. As the first letter to appear in the Torah, the open side of the *bet* is followed by the words that narrate the creation and history of the world (Gen. 1:1 *folio*). This interpretation also effectively offers a counter-interpretation to a famous Midrash which cautions against pursuing the secrets of cosmology, the afterlife, and cosmogony—"R. Jonah said in R. Levi's name: Why was the world created with a *bet*? Just as the *bet* is closed at the sides but open in front, so you are not permitted to investigate what is above and what below, what is before . . . " (*Gen. R.* 1:10)—an attitude wholly contradictory to the spirit of the *Bahir.*

2. House of the cosmos. The interpretation is playing on the fact that the physical shape of the letter *bet* is derived from a pictograph of a house (*bayit* in Hebrew). Both time and space flow from it.

3. God is the place of the world, but the world is not His place. This quote from a famous and oft-repeated Midrash (*Gen. R.* 69:8) is the classical statement of Jewish panentheism: the universe is wholly within God, all things participate in divinity, but God is greater still than the sum of the universe. This alternative to classic theism becomes one of the central pillars of Kabbalah.

4. So don't read it as. *Al tikra* "don't read it as X, but as Y" is a famous rabbinic hermeneutic, which exploits the ambiguity regarding the meaning of words and phrases resulting from the fact that classical Hebrew lacks vowels. It is used in many homilies to confirm an interpretive point which might not otherwise be obvious.

5. A house is built with wisdom [and established

by understanding]. i.e., the "house" of the cosmos flows from *Chochmah*, "wisdom," and *Binah*, "understanding," two of the highest *Sefirot*. This teaching is intended to establish both the letter/word mysticism and the sefirotic system of the earlier esoteric work, *Sefer Yetzirah,* are cryptically confirmed by the Hebrew Bible itself; *sodot,* "secrets" occulted in the teaching of the Bible and the early rabbis. Every "house"(relationship, family, society, the world) thrives only if standing on a foundation of wisdom and insight.

GEOFFREY W. DENNIS

THE CORNUCOPIA OF GOOD
§20(M); §13(S-A)

Why does the *gimel* have a tail?
To teach that the top of the *gimel* is On High,1
So it resembles a cornucopia, like the concluding
  [letter] *nun.*2
Just as a channel conveys from above to below,
So too, the *gimel* conveys the way [of divine
  goodness] from the top,3
and releases it by way of the tail,4
and thus, "*gimel.*"5

RELATED BIBLICAL TEXT:

**I will sing to YHVH for bestowing good upon me
(Ps. 13:6).**

1. The top of the *gimel* is on high. Gimel is the third letter of the Hebrew alphabet, the consonant "G." The shape of the *gimel* (ג) imitates, indeed, embodies, its cosmic function. Its top resides in the higher worlds.

2. So it resembles a cornucopia. Literally, "channel," but the sense is that the shape conveys goodness and divine sustenance, hence the English "cornucopia" better captures the connotation intended in this teaching. The main body of the letter resembles a vertical pipe, or a channel, similar to shape of the *nun sofit,* the letter *nun* as it appears at the end of a Hebrew word. The *nun sofit* symbolizes the human soul, the *neshamah* which, unbent by sin, reaches from Earth to heaven (*Otiyot Rabbi Akiva*).

3. The way [of divine goodness]. The teaching elides what precisely is being conveyed for now, but the wordplay at the end reveals it to the discerning.

4. Releases it by way of the tail. The divine bounty, represented by the *alef* in the earlier teaching, pours into the lower worlds by means of this conduit.

5. And thus, *"gimel."* This obscure conclusion assumes the reader will be able to decode the *polysemy* at work here. The word for the letter, *gimel,* contains the same consonants as the verb *gamal,* "bestow," to grant something good upon a recipient without expectation of reward or compensation. Jews will be familiar with the divine commandment of *gimilut chasidim,* to bestow loving-kindness upon others. What God does for us, we are to do likewise, for this commandment is understood to be a mimesis of what God regularly does for Creation.

GEOFFREY W. DENNIS

THE SOUND OF THE SOUL,
A HEALING JEWEL
§40-41(M); 27 (S-A)

His [R. Amor's] students asked him, "What is a
   cholam?" 1
He replied, it is the soul, and its name is *cholam.*
   2
If you hearken to it, it will heal your body in the
   future-to-come,3
But if you rebel against it, illness will return to
   your head, 4
and sickness to its head.5
And furthermore, he said, every dream is in the
   cholam, 6
and every white jewel is in the *chalam,* 7
as it is written, . . . and a crystal (Ex. 28:19).8

RELATED BIBLICAL TEXT:

**A great God has made known to the king what
shall be after this. The dream is certain, and its
interpretation sure (Daniel 2:45).**

1. **"What is a *cholam?*"** The *cholam* is the Hebrew vowel for Ō. It is represented either by a dot (ao) superscription, or using the consonant *vav* with the dot on top (uuA). The latter shape will factor into the complex teaching that follows, which links the *cholam* to three entities, all based on wordplay.

2. **It is the soul.** The Hebrew word for soul used here, *nashamah,* is the highest level of the Jewish scheme of the manifold human soul (See § 8/4). This association is likely inspired by the Pythagorean and Gnostic belief that the vowel sounds are celestial entities. Specifically, this appears linked to the Gnostic text Masanes, which holds that the vowels are the "shapes" of the primary, or highest, souls.

3. **If you hearken to it.** Following the dictates of soul ensures a desirable future incarnation. This is an oblique reference to the doctrine of reincarnation (§121/86). The phrase *atid lavo* (future to come) is perhaps meant here as a synonym for the more common *olam ha-ba* (World-to-Come) (T. *Arachin* 2:7). But while the latter refers to the final resting place of the soul, here the former is meant to convey something else, the death of Death; the next stage of the soul's journey *(B. M. K. 28b).*

4. **Illness will return to your head**. A word play: *cholim,* "sick ones." You will fail to advance in incarnations toward the messianic future.

5. **And sickness to its head.** The soul, symbolized by the dot over the *vav* of the *cholam,* will wither.

6. **Every dream is in the *cholam*.** A second wordplay: *chalom,* "dream." All dreams emanate from the soul, making them a kind of divine revelation.

7. **Every white jewel is in the *chalam*.** A third wordplay. This is the most enigmatic passage. First, this is the only place the root *ch-l-m* is spelled without the vowel *cholam* actually appearing in the word. This may be a simple scribal error, or it is more likely meant to convey the secondary meaning of *chalam,* "vision." The puzzle is the relationship and the significance of "vision," to the gem, to the soul.

8. **And a crystal.** "Crystal" in Hebrew, *achlamah*, has the same linguistic root as *cholam* and *chalom*. This briefest of biblical proof texts refers to the *achlamah* stone that is one of the twelve gems arrayed on the divinatory breastplate (*choshen mishpat*) of the High Priest. The breastplate itself is a mantic device (*Ex.* 28:30; *B. Yoma* 73b), so perhaps the author is simply confirming that dreams are a kind of lesser prophecy (*B. Ber.* 57b). Perhaps the author is alluding to the Bible commentator Ibn Ezra's claiming this *achlamah* is an amethyst, a gemstone credited with inducing dreams (his comment to Lev. 28:19). The Talmud also holds that gems have curative powers (*B. Sanh.* 68a), linking this back to lines 3-5. So the essence is this: the vowel-letter *cholam* signifies the soul, the divine aspect of humanity which possesses the power to heal and to perceive the future.

GEOFFREY W. DENNIS

HAY IS THE PORTAL TO THE WORLD TO COME
§8 (M); §4 (S-A)

Why did the Holy One of blessing
Add a *hay* to [the name of] Abraham,1
in preference to any other letter?
In order that all the limbs of a man
should merit life in the World to Come,2
which is likened to the sea.3
It is as if—if one could say such a thing—
the building [of humanity] was completed in
   him.4
As it is written, **For in the image of God He made
   the human** (Gen. 9:6).5
And in Gematria, "Abraham" equals
the number of limbs in a human.6

RELATED BIBLICAL TEXT:

***Let Us make humanity in Our image* (Gen. 1:26)**

1. **Add a *hay*.** *Gen.* 17:5, where God changes Avram's name to Avraham. The letter *hay* (h) appears twice in YHVH, the most sacred name of God, and is often used as a metonym for God's name.

2. **Merit the World to Come.** This letter, by means of its cosmic potency, grants humanity a closer kinship to divinity.

3. **Which is likened to the sea.** It is unclear why this comparison is included here. Perhaps it is a reference to *Job.* 11:7-9, where the mystery or essence of God is described as "broader than the sea." The comparison of the World to Come to the sea also appears in *Eccl. R.* 1:36. Elsewhere, we have seen the word "sea" used to signify "Torah" (§3/3, §96/65).

4. **The building was completed in him.** Abraham achieved a level of human excellence that prior worthies, such as Adam, Enoch, and Noah, could not.

5. **For in the image of God He made the human.** The choice of this verse is deliberate. The phrase "image of God" is repeated four times (Gen. 1:26, 27; 5:1; 9:6) before the appearance of Abraham. *Gen. R.* 14:9 speaks of the soul having five "names," later interpreted as five levels. This means to suggest that over the generations since Adam, God has been gradually adding dimensions to the human soul, and with the addition of "*hay*," a letter from the divine name with the not-so-coincidental number value "5," the five-level soul is now complete, and humanity can fully participate in the eternality of divinity. It should be noted that prior to the rise of Kabbalah, most Jewish texts claimed the human soul was only tri-fold.

6. **"Abraham" equals the number of limbs.** The numerical value of the Hebrew letters in Abraham's name

is 248, which elsewhere the Sages say is the number of parts that make up the human body (*B. Oholot* 1:8). Moreover, 2+4+8=14; 1+4=5! Thus Abraham was the first person since the loss of the Garden of Eden to actually embody the physical and psychic potential God envisioned for humanity from the first. He is like a new Adam. Less obvious, *hay* is the image of God. How so? The shape itself reveals that God cannot look up, for there is nothing above divinity, cannot look to the sides, as there is no place outside divinity, but can only look "down," into the creation unfolding "below."

The Tree of Life: Bridge Between Heaven and Earth

Introduction

THE "TREE OF LIFE" or "world tree" is a symbol that enjoys iconic status within cultures across time and across the planet. It serves as a metonymy for all life; as a bridge that links heaven, the earth, and underworld; functions as the pillar that upholds heaven; and is emblematic of the intertwined, life-sustaining natural order. The image of the "sacred tree" makes its first appearance in Mesopotamian art in the fourth millennium, BCE. By the 1st century of the Common Era, the symbol has permeated the art of cultures from Greece to the Indus valley. In most of these cultures, the tree serves as an embodiment of the divine order, or a map of the macrocosm.[8]

A significant contribution the *Bahir* makes to the development of Judaism is how it revitalizes and expands earlier Israelite mythic symbols, like the Throne of Glory envisioned in Isaiah chapter 6, or the primordial chaos described in Genesis. It does this by imbuing these symbols with new associations and deeper philosophical meaning. Consider the primordial Tree of Life, mentioned only twice in the book of Gen. Yet the Tree continues in the Jewish imagination in a variety of forms. The Book of Proverbs explicitly links it to Wisdom, which is treated as an almost divine entity. The Rabbis then equate the Tree with the Torah, another entity imbued with God's power, making it a divine gift which we lost when we were expelled from Eden but regained at Mount Sinai.

The *Bahir* embraces all these associations but goes on to say that the Tree of Life, or the All Tree, is the first of God's creations, the Center, or pivot, of the World (*Axis Mundi*), and, elaborating on the minimal description found in an earlier esoteric text, *Sefer Yetzirah*, the *Sefirot*, moving toward a great cosmic "unified theory" of divine involvement and presence in creation. The image of the All Tree presents the world as a vast, intertwining living entity made up of all matter, words, numbers, and living things. Most important, the arboreal metaphor of the Tree conveys the insight that the material and spiritual worlds not only intersect, they infuse each other, creating a new vision of the *Malei*, "Fullness," a term the *Bahir* uses repeatedly. The result is that the *Bahir* inspires a renewed sense of the mythological into Jewish thinking, formulating a symbol-rich rhetoric of describing Judaism that re-enchants it and inspires its followers. Consequently, because of the *Bahir*, the Tree will become ever more iconic and will undergo constant elaboration by subsequent generations of Kabbalists, like Isaac ha-Kohen, Moses deLeon, and Isaac Luria. In time, the Tree of Life will be absorbed into Christian and Western esoteric traditions still alive today. Thus the Jewish Tree of Life is a bridge, not only a symbolic spiritual bridge between heaven and Earth but a historical bridge linking the intellectual world of the ancient near east to that of the modern western mind.

In the four sections devoted to this theme, *First There was All* presents an unconventional interpretation of the primordial created entities that first emanated from the One. *The Waters of Life* teaches that God anticipates what the created world will require to survive, using the metaphor of a gardener and garden. *The Tree that is All* teaches that the "Tree of Life" serves as a kind of cosmic scaffolding for all creation, and in *The Tree and the Fountainhead,* we will read about the divine process of its creation, its preeminent place in the order of being, its centrality, and something of its metaphysics, much of it couched in archly metaphoric arboreal imagery.

Texts found in other sections of this collection which have related content: §20(M); §13 (S-A); §80-81(M); §54-55 (S-A)

First There Was All
§10(M); §8(S-A)

The Torah said: I was first to be, the beginning of the world,1
as it is written, **From of old I was fashioned, from the first** (Proverbs 8:23).2
If you were to say the earth preceded it, it is written . . . preceding the earth (ibid.).
It is as it was written, **With the beginning [He] created God, the heaven and the earth** (*Gen. 1:1*).3
What is "created?" He created all the needs of the All.4
[only] Afterwards, "God." 5
And what is written after that? "The heaven and the earth."6

Related Biblical Text:

Adonai brought me forth as the beginning of his ways, before his deeds of old; from of old I was fashioned, from the first, preceding the earth (Prov. 8:22-23).

1. Torah said: I was first. This follows the influential Midrash (*Gen. R.* 1.1) that describes Torah as both God's architect and blueprint for the world. As the Torah is the ultimate repository of supernal letters and words, this teaching expands on the metaphysics discussed in Section 2. What follows is an argument that even Hebrew syntax contains secret revelations.

2. I was fashioned. In the Proverbs, Wisdom, personified as a dignified woman, is speaking. The Rabbis equate Wisdom with Torah (see §3/3).

3. The Beginning . . . created God. This unconventional, but nonetheless valid, translation reflects the word order in Hebrew. This reading is critical to what follows.

4. The needs of the All. The "All" here refers to the Tree of Life, or All Tree, which is Wisdom/Torah, as we shall see (§22/14). Throughout the *Bahir*, various Jewish, Near Eastern, and Mediterranean traditions about the entities that make up the *Pleroma,* the "Divine fullness"—the angelic order, heavenly palaces, divine attributes, numbers, and powers—are being brought together and equated with one another. These are the real first emanation from the *Ein Sof*, the Boundless, or Infinite One, the essence of God. Together, the *Bahir* teaches, these constitute the "Tree of Life" that sustains our existence in the material universe.

5. Created God. This renders the Hebrew of *Gen.* 1:1 hyper-literally as "With the beginning He created *Elohim* . . . " In this reading, "beginning" is Torah, as established by Prov. 8:22. But who is the subject who created with Torah? The "He" is an implied part of the third-person singular verb "created" in Hebrew, so, even in the absence of a direct object marker, because of word order, "God" is treated as

the first object rather than the subject of the sentence. The author claims the *Ein Sof*, the ineffable Deity, emanated the All Tree/Wisdom/Torah first, and only then manifested *Elohim,* which we conventionally translate as "God" but is understood here to be only that aspect of Divinity which manifests order, law, and judgment. This mirrors the Platonic concept of the demiurge, the secondary divinity that is the creative force of the cosmos. The rather startling idea that the God of the Bible is actually a subsidiary entity, a secondary manifestation of the unknowable Infinite, will become a major feature of Jewish mysticism. Thus the Tree of Life is the *Axis Mundi,* the cosmic navel of this unfolding, from which the infinite shifts into the finite and the indefinable coalesce into graspable categories of spiritual and material reality.

6. And what is written after that? This also alludes to the Hebrew syntactical particle "*et*" (ta), which appears in front of both the word "heaven" and "Earth." Linguistically, this is known as a "direct object indicator." The author, however, seems to be treating it as an esoteric merism: since *et* consists of *alef* and *tav,* the first and last letters of the alphabet, it is being interpreted to mean "all things between *alef* and *tav*," or more simply, "everything/all" (B. T. *Pes.* 22b).

THE WATERS OF LIFE
§23(M); §15(S-A)

Rabbi Rachumai said,
From your words [the words of Rabbi Yochanan,
   on the order of creation] we learn
that the Holy One of blessing created the need of
   this world prior to heaven.1
He said thus, a parable: To what may this be
   compared?
To a king that desired to plant a tree in his garden.
He searched the entire garden to see if there was
   a bubbling spring of water.
[When] he found nothing, he said,
"I will dig for water
And I will find a spring,
in order that I will be able to sustain the tree."
He dug and he brought forth a bubbling spring
From a source of living water,2
So afterward he planted the tree.3
Then it stood and produced fruit
And its roots grew strong, for they replenished it
   continuously
with what was drawn from the spring.4

RELATED BIBLICAL TEXT:

*By Wisdom YHVH has founded the earth; He
established the heavens by Understanding. By
His Knowledge, the depths were split open, and
the dusts drip dew (Prov. 3:19).*

1. The Holy One of blessing created the need of this world prior to heaven. This is the last in a series of debates the *Bahir* records about the order of creation, a debate going back centuries in Jewish metaphysics. This seemingly pedantic question actually carries important implications: which is more important in the divine scheme, the heavens, with its celestial hierarchy (the transcendent *Pleroma*) or the world with its flesh-and-blood creatures (the imminent)? Alternately, if the "Earth" here is a symbol for the Divine Throne, as it is in a previous teaching, then this deliberately reverses the priority of creation from §22/14, suggesting both are equally important, neither precedes the other. The phrase "created the *need* of this world" has the sense of "what the world needs," as discussed in §10/8.

2. From a source of living water. Wisdom (Prov. 3:19).

3. Afterward he planted the tree. The "All Tree," which encompasses the universe and links the upper and lower worlds (see §22/14, following).

4. Then it stood and produced fruit. It made possible the celestial and lower realms. The parable is awkward, given its topic of cosmogony. A king of flesh and blood, who seeks and discovers but does not invent, seems a poor parallel for Divine creativity; it is almost more like a Jungian dream than a parable. And it lacks an explicit *nimshal*/explanation. It would seem to put forward a surprising claim; that wisdom also sustains the order on high, and without it, heaven and the angels could not thrive. The embodied world is actually a critically important aspect of God's plan, for life, infused with wisdom, sustains the divine *Pleroma*, rather than the heavens wholly sustaining the world, as is the perspective of classical theism. Ultimately, however, this cryptic teaching evades complete clarification, inviting the reader to impose a preferred meaning.

THE TREE THAT IS ALL
§22(M); §14(S-A)

**I Adonai make all; I alone stretch out the sky, the
    earth spreads out from Me** (Is. 44:24).
[Read the last word as] **Who is with me?**1
I [alone] am the one that planted this tree for all
    the world to delight in it.2
And through it I spread all.
I called its name All, 3
for everything depends on it,
everything goes forth from it,
everything requires it, looks to it, waits for it,
and from there the souls blossom in joy.4
I was alone when I made it.
No angel excels above it who can say "I preceded
    you!"5
I was also alone when I spread out my earth in
    which I planted and rooted this tree.6
I rejoiced in [their] unification and I rejoiced in
    them,
**Who was with me that I revealed to him this
    mystery?**7

RELATED BIBLICAL TEXT:

***She is a Tree** of Life for those who embrace her,
and whoever holds on to her is happy* **(Prov.
3:18).**

1. Who is with me? In Hebrew, a minor emendation of the text renders the last word *mi eeti* rather than *meiti*. This seems aimed to contradict any claim for a primordial entity that coexisted with God before creation.

2. This tree. The Tree of Life (Gen. 2:9; Prov. 3:18), which here is also the *Sefirot*, the ten divine powers through which all reality emerges.

3. I called its name All. The Tree is the totality of all there is. All created consciousness is connected to it.

4. Souls blossom in joy. A wordplay. The Hebrew *porekh* can mean "bloom" or "fly." The arboreal image is intuitive here. The Human soul is the fruit of the Tree. On the other hand, the avian reading links this to birds (usually doves) as totems of the human soul. In another passage on the Tree (§119/85), the same verb is used but with the "flying" of souls emphasized.

5. No angel excels above it. The Tree takes priority over all celestial, as well as earthly, reality. This passage seeks to subsume earlier Jewish angelology within the Tree of Life/*Sefirot* motif.

6. My earth in which I planted . . . this tree. Elsewhere (§96/65), "earth" is revealed to be a code word for the Throne of Glory, which the Rabbis characterized as the concretized symbol of divine sovereignty, the substrate of reality. These two pre-existent entities, earth and tree, sovereignty and life-force, form the ground of being. There is a discernible sexual symbolism, with the tree as the masculine principle and the earth the feminine. This carries through to the next line, which refers to the "unification" of the two.

7. Who was with me? This alludes to the rhetorical question God poses to Job at the beginning of the "Creator speech": "Where were you when I laid the earth's foundations?" (Job 38:4). The rest of God's revelatory poem (Job 38:5-41:26) becomes an elaborate coda to this section.

GEOFFREY W. DENNIS

THE TREE AND THE FOUNTAINHEAD
§119(M); §85(S-A)

What this Tree that you speak of?
He said to him, [It is the] powers of the Holy One of
blessing,
one atop another, so they resemble a tree.1
Just as a tree, by water[ing], yields fruit, so too the Holy
One of blessing
multiplies the powers of the Tree by water[ing].
And what is the 'water' of the Holy One of blessing?
It is Wisdom, and the souls of the righteous fly forth2
From the fountainhead toward the great channel,
ascend and cleave to the Tree. And by what means do they
fly?
By means of Israel,3
for when they are righteous and good,
the *Shekhinah* dwells in their midst,4
and through their deeds they dwell in the bosom of the
Holy One of blessing.5
He makes them fruitful and causes them to multiple.6

RELATED BIBLICAL TEXT:

**And he shall be like a tree planted by streams of
water, that brings forth its fruit in its season (Ps.
1:3)**

1. It is the powers of the Holy One of blessing. The *Sefirot*. This allusion also serves as a fitting transition to the next section.

2. The souls of the righteous fly forth. In §22/14, the image was of all souls blooming/flying forth from the Tree. Here, the image is reciprocal: wisdom flows "down" the conduit of the Tree, and in response, the souls of the righteous soar "upward" to nest in various branches of the Tree.

3. The sacred communion of Israel serves as the fountainhead, the source of wisdom below that propels the ascent.

4. The Shekhinah dwells in their midst. The Divine Presence. Alluding to Ex. 25:8 (See §102/71). Elsewhere, she personifies righteousness (§75M), the quality that allows her to dwell with the people.

5. They dwell in the bosom of the Holy One of blessing. Through moral and ritual perfection, Israel becomes one with the Godhead. A cosmic union is realized at several levels.

6. He makes them fruitful and multiples them. The deeds of the righteous magnify God's presence but also multiply righteousness itself, sustaining the tree from below. The language of fruitfulness alludes both to the procreative blessing of primordial humanity (Gen. 1:28) and the cosmic potency of wisdom (Ps. 1:3) that the Tree embodies.

SEFIROT:
DIVINE NUMBERS,
DIVINE EMANATIONS

THE MOST ENDURING contribution of the *Bahir* is its contribution to the development of the mystical doctrine of the *Sefirot*, ten emanations, divine qualities or attributes, which are the substrate of all creation.[9] The word *sefirah* (pl. *Sefirot*) first appears in an earlier esoteric text, the *Sefer Yetzirah* ("The Book of Formation"). *Sefirah* most likely means "numeral," and in *Sefer Yetzirah*, the *Sefirot* are the numbers one through ten that, with the twenty-two letters of the Hebrew alphabet, constitute the "thirty-two paths of wisdom," the building blocks with which God creates the universe. The *Sefer Yetzirah* itself doesn't go much beyond the (important) idea that numbers can give us useful insight into the structures of nature.

Sefer ha-Bahir takes the idea of the *Sefirot* in a radically new direction. By combining the numeric thinking of *Sefer Yetzirah* with a separate Rabbinic teaching that God created the world by means of ten utterances (*ma'amarot*), the *Bahir* begins to shape a much richer notion of the *Sefirot* as multifaceted and dynamic representations of divine wisdom, will, and order. That being said, *Bahiric* notions of the *Sefirot* are quite fluid and open-ended, no doubt in part because the multiple authors held different perspectives on this emerging metaphysical model. And it cannot be emphasized enough: different discrete teachings of the *Bahir* offer tidbits of contradictory systems, as well as teachings that labor strenuously to reconcile the ten *Sefirot* with earlier metaphysical models involving angelic forces, the Tree of Life, or prior traditions which identify the divine powers with the sacred numbers seven or three.

But this process of integration also yields a rich vocabulary of symbols associated with the divine emanations. We will see this in the many iconic images and metaphors the *Bahir* uses to characterize the divine powers: light, Torah, God's Throne of Glory, the sea, jewels, and the Tree of Life.

Later interpreters of the *Bahir* would attempt to visualize the *Sefirot* in a more systematic way. Here are three examples:

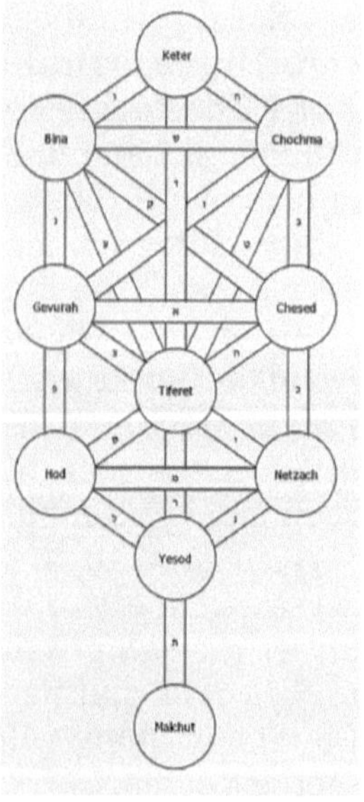

[Fig. 1 GRA "tree"]

[Fig. 2 Cordovero Letters]

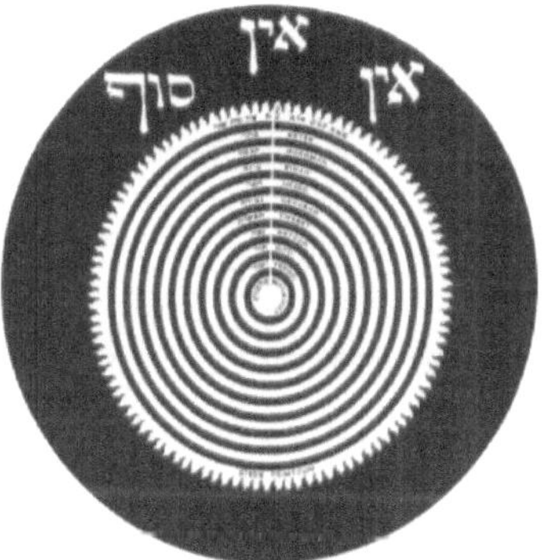

[Fig. 3 Luria Concentric Circles]

It is not self-evident that the authors of the *Bahir* yet envisioned the *Sefirot* specifically in any of these ways, nor is every symbol in the *Bahir* alluding to the *Sefirot*, but the seeds for all these interpretations can be found in the book. As one can sense, the *Sefirot,* as expounded ("described" being too precise), and the *Bahir* are on their way to becoming yet another iconic way for the mystic to understand the divine *Pleroma.*

Texts not included in this section but which have related content: §27(M); §19; §124(M); §87 (S-A).

GEOFFREY W. DENNIS

THE PARABLE OF THE MUSTARD SEED
§179 (M); §122 (S-A)

We have learned,
'There are ten spheres and ten Utterances'1
Each and every sphere has an Utterance.
It is not surrounded by it, but it surrounds the
  other.2
This world can be compared to a mustard seed in
  a ploughed field.3
How so? Because of the moisture that blows upon
  it,4
And so it is sustained. And if the moisture should
  stop
for even a minute, the world would wither.5

RELATED RABBINIC TEXT:

**The world was created in ten utterances (M. Avot
5:1).**

1. Ten spheres and ten Utterances. Since ancient times, the sphere has been considered the most perfect, most divine shape (Empedocles). One pre-Socratic thinker, Xenophanes, even believed that God was sphere-shaped. The decimal-number system arises intuitively as the most logical because of human physiology, as well as appearing as a sacred number in the Torah. The Ten Utterances are the ten times the phrase "And God said" appears in the account of Creation (Gen. 1,2; *Avot* 5:1).

2. But it surrounds the other. A confusing burst of pronouns, but the essence is: the "word" is contained in the sphere. If the next sentence is even close to correct, this is correct.

3. **Mustard seed in a ploughed field.** The meaning is doubtful. Different manuscripts have radically different versions, starting here. The best this author can extract is a simple parable. The Word of God is the seed, and the spheres are the medium in which it grows. In the parables of Jesus, he compares the Kingdom of God to a mustard seed (Mark 4:30-32).

4. **The moisture that blows upon it.** Alternately, "the wind that blows upon it." In either case, the point seems to be the moisture/wind is the divine emanating forces that flow through the spheres, serving as the catalyst for a living cosmos.

5. **For even a minute, the world would wither.** The parable is abruptly abandoned; the seed becomes the world, and the message is that without the constant flow of the divine spirit/emanation/effluence, the Word could not be realized. This text appears to be corrupted in transmission, but something of the point emerges nonetheless. The ten "spheres," the *Sefirot*, are the matrix from which the world unfolds, but the whole system

depends on continued divine engagement to sustain it. Maintaining that flow, closing any breaches, this is the task of the enlightened who understand the divine economy.

-91-

GEOFFREY W. DENNIS

THE PARABLE OF THE TEN KINGS
§27(M); 19(S-A)

His [Rabbi Amorai's] students asked him,
"What is the letter *dalet*?"[1]
He said to them,
It may be compared to ten kings in a single place.[2]
All of them were wealthy,
But one among the ten was not wealthy like the
  others.[3]
Even though he was very wealthy,
he was called "poor" relative to the others.[4]

RELATED BIBLICAL TEXT:

*He raises the poor from the dust and lifts the
needy from the ash heap; he seats them with
princes and has them inherit a throne of honor.
For the foundations of the earth are YHVH's; on
them He has set the world (I Sam. 2:8).*

1. What is the letter *dalet*? The fourth letter of the Hebrew *alef-bet*, it symbolizes the consonant "D." The word *delet* also means "door." The question here is: what is its cosmological import? Because all letters are cosmic forces. This teaching is part of a longer passage of teacher-student exchanges regarding the alphabet.

2. Ten kings in a single place. The ten *Sefirot* that give form to and govern the universe. A very minimalist parable.

3. One among the ten was not wealthy like the others. One of the divine potencies lacks an attribute possessed by the others. While the parable lacks a proper *nimshal* to identify the poor king, given the context of the *Bahir* in its entirety, this is most likely referring to the divine power, later identified as *Malchut/Shekhinah*. One clue to guide on this is that *Shekhinah* does not emanate like the other *Sefirot* but only receives [like our parabolic king, it is "poor"] (see §156/104). Prior to the *Bahir*, the *Shekhinah* is more simply characterized as the "indwelling" Presence, or imminent aspect of God. The term is derived from Ex. 25:8. In subsequent Kabbalah, this term comes to be *the* idiom for the feminine aspect of God, a concept that appears multiple times elsewhere in the *Bahir*. Note, however, that in the parable, this "king" is not treated as feminine as *Shekhinah* is elsewhere. This may reflect that the author of this particular passage has not yet settled upon assigning all feminine attributes of God to the feminine word *Shekhinah*.

4. **He was called "poor" relative to the others.** This is a Hebrew wordplay on *dalet,* which contains the word *dal*, "poor." Under the influence of the *Bahir*, the *Shekhinah* is more complex, more paradoxical than the other *sefirot*, it is both poor and fabulously rich, and while it is interpreted as "passive" and "lower" than the others

(see §172/116), it is also the most beloved and, in fact, the most essential force in the divine order (see §54/36). This two-fold nature of the divine feminine, lowly but beloved, will become the most essential idea of the emerging kabbalistic teachings. God's special love for the lowly and deprived is a theme that goes back to the Bible (Job 5;11; Ps. 147:6).

GEOFFREY W. DENNIS

THE HIGHEST CROWN
§141(M); §96(S-A)

What are the Ten Utterances?1
The first is the highest crown.2
Blessed and praised be His name and *Its* people.
And who are Its people?3
Israel, as it is written, **Know that YHVH is God.**
   He made us His people
and we are for It (Ps. 100:3).
The verse [literally] reads, **we are for** *alef.*4
To recognize and know the One of Ones, the Unity
   in all His names.5

RELATED BIBLICAL TEXT:

**And God said, "let there be light," and behold,
there was light. (Gen. 1:5).**

1. What are the Ten Utterances? According to the Talmud, God utters ten speech-acts (*ma'amarot*) in *Gen.* chapters 1 and 2 (T. B. *Avot* 5:1;*B. R.H.* 32a). The *Bahir* correlates this ancient teaching with the concept of the ten *Sefirot* (see §141).

2. The first is the Highest Crown. *Alef*, the first and silent letter, corresponds with God's first and highest thought, the one that was not spoken (See §70/48), which was expressed in the biblical verse, **In the beginning, God created the heaven and the earth** (Gen. 1:1). This first "utterance" is closest to the unfathomable reality of the unbounded and ineffable God. In other kabbalistic writings, the "Highest Crown," *keter elyon*, initiates the creation *ex nihilo,* the formation of something from nothing, the gesture that, according to the medieval rationalist philosophers, demonstrates God's status as Supreme Being, since there was no pre-existent matter to work with.

3. Its people. This pronoun is normally translated "for His," but the *Bahir* notes that here, the spelling of the Hebrew word *lo* is anomalous, ending with an *alef,* the letter signifying God's first thought. This contains an occult revelation: the people are uniquely linked the fountainhead of God's creative impulse.

4. We are for *alef.* Israel is bound to the highest of divine emanations.

5. The Unity in all His names. The One who lies at the root of all attributes, potencies, and *Sefirot*. The Jewish people are bound to this root power and are required to understand God in a manner unlike other peoples.

THE SABBATH SUSTAINS ALL OF THEM
§157-158(M); §104 (S-A)

But is it not written,
Then on the seventh day, He rested, *y'ninafah*
   (Ex. 31:17)?2
Surely, it is the seventh [utterance], for it divides
   them.3
The six Utterances, three below and three above.
And for what reason is it called the "seventh?"4
Did it exist only on the seventh day?
No, rather, [because] the Holy One of blessing
   rested on the Sabbath.5
Of that attribute it is written,
Six days YHVH made the heaven and the earth,
then on the seventh day, He rested, *y'ninafah*.
Teaching that all days have their Utterance that
   rules them.6
This is not because [that power] was created on
   that day,
Rather, because He worked [that day] using its
   power.
Each worked its power and transmitted His deeds.
Therefore the seventh comes and performs its
   power,
Which is to cheer them all; even the Holy One of
   blessing.
Not only that, but it enlarges their souls, as it is
   written,
then on the seventh day, He rested, *v'yinafash*.7

1. *Y'ninafah.* "And He was refreshed." Literally, "and He was re-souled." The Hebrew is so critical to the interpretation that follows I left it untranslated in the text.

2. It is the seventh [utterance], for it divides them. As we have seen in the preceding passages, most of the Bahir builds on the rabbinic teaching of the Ten Utterances. Strangely and unexpectedly, this rejects the model of ten divine powers entirely, arguing there are only seven potencies, represented in the days of creation, or perhaps the seven heavens familiar to Jews from Greco-Roman times. Here, the six powers/days revolve around the seventh, the Sabbath, which is the *axis mundi* and most powerful of them all.

3. **And for what reason is it called the "seventh?"** If it occupies the "dividing" position, should it not be the "fourth" power (three before, three after)?

4. **The Holy One of blessing rested on the Sabbath.** It pre-existed the creative process, but God did not deploy this most-powerful potency until the last day, making it the "seventh."

5. **All days have their Utterance that rules them.** The seven *ma'amarot* (divine Utterances or Logoi) are not the six days of creation in themselves, but they all became manifest with each day.

6. **Even the Holy One of blessing.** It sustains even the Godhead. And that particular power causes all "souls to grow," suggesting this is the same potency as the All Tree and the Foundation described in §§ 22/14 and 184/126. But for the modern reader, the most surprising discovery might be that this idea of heptahedronal, seven-based, divine powers is pretty much unique to the *Bahir,* with no true parallels appearing in prior Jewish interpretive

RELATED BIBLICAL TEXT:

For six days work may be done, but on the seventh day there is a Sabbath of complete rest, a holy convocation (Lev. 23:3).

tradition. At the same time, as scholars Shlomo Pines and Elliot Wolfson have pointed out, a very similar teaching *does* appear in the early Judeo-Christian text, Pseudo-Clementine *Homilies* 17, IX-X. In the *Homilies*, Christ is the *Axis Mundi*/Sabbath/Foundation/source of souls in a metaphysic of seven divine powers. It seems likely, therefore, that this interpretation (and possibly others) in the *Bahir* has been repurposed from a Jewish-Christian source for a Jewish audience, their Christological associations removed.

THE PARABLE OF THE SEVEN SONS
§172(M); §116 (S-A)

He sat and expounded to them,
"Just as [there is] the Shekhinah above,
So too, She is below.1yes
And what is this Shekhinah?
He said, "This is light emanating from the first
   light, which is Wisdom.2
It surrounds everything, as it is written,
The whole earth is full of His Glory (Is. 6:3).3
What is its function here?
A parable of a king who had seven sons 4
And each and every one had his place.
He said to them, "Dwell here, one over the other."
The one at the bottom said, "I will not dwell below,
   or so distant from you."
He said, "I surround you all, and see you all,
   daily."
And why is he among them?5
In order to support them and sustain them.6
And what are these sons?
I have told you before, the Holy One of blessing
Has seven holy forms.7
All of them correspond in humanity.8
As it is written, **For in the image of God He made
   him** (Gen. 9:6).

RELATED BIBLICAL TEXT:

***Do not cast me from Your presence or take your
Holy Spirit from me* (Ps. 51:11).**

1. The Shekhinah. The "indwelling" Presence. Yet despite the fact that the noun *shekhinah* is a feminine noun, this teaching makes no explicit effort to connect *Shekhinah* with the female in deity, as the parable that follows demonstrates.

2. The first light, which is Wisdom. This weaves together two important earlier teachings about the creation of the world: that God used hypostatic Wisdom as the template for its creation (Prov. 8:22; *Gen. R.* 1.1) and that there was a primordial light that pre-existed visible light (Ps. 97:11; *Gen. R.* 3.6; *Lev. R.* 11:17). To put it in an English idiom, the first "light" that God created (Gen. 1:2) was "enlightenment."

3. His Glory. *Kavod* is the biblical word for the divine presence. Here, we are being instructed that *Kavod* and *Shekhinah* are synonymous.

4. Seven sons. Most interpreters take this to be a reference to the *Sefirot,* though there are only seven rather than the ten mentioned elsewhere. Such interpreters adopt the position that this refers to the seven "lower" *Sefirot* that project into positive existence, but it may be this particular contributor to the *Bahir* is expounding an alternate paradigm in which there are only seven powers, as discussed in §157-158/ §104.

5. And why is he among them? Why is there simultaneously a *Shekhinah* above and below? This is the beginning of the *nimshal,* the explanation of the parable.

6. To support them and sustain them. These emanations, while of God, are not God and need constant divine sustenance. This mirrors the Mu`tazilite philosophy of early Islam that insisted God must consciously intervene at all levels of existence for existence to continue. The

Rabbis make the same point in the prayer *Yotzer Ohr,* "Shaper of Light": "You renew the work of creation, daily, constantly."

7. The Holy One of blessing has seven holy forms. The word used here is *tzorot,* which echoes the platonic world of Forms (*Sophist* 246-259; *Phdr.* 247c). Elsewhere in the *Bahir*, we see teachings that reconcile competing traditions of the sacred ten and the sacred seven.

8. All of them correspond in humanity. Just as there is *Shekhinah* above and below, all the divine potencies above have corresponding forms below, embodied in the human form (see §82/§55).

Geoffrey W. Dennis

The Mystery of
the Great Holy Ones
§125-126(M); §87-88 (S-A)

And why are they called *Sefirot*?1
Because it is written, **The heavens recount the Glory of God** (Ps. 19:2).2
And what are they?
They are three,3
And they include three hosts and three dominions. 4
The first dominion is light,
And light is the life of water.5
The second dominion is the holy beasts, the ofanim, the wheels of the chariot,6
And all the troops of the Holy One of blessing,
[that] praise, proclaim, glorify, laud, and sanctify
the king surrounded in holiness7
and exulted through the mystery of the great holy ones,8
a king fearsome and awesome,
so they crown him with three "holys."9

Related Biblical Text:

***Yours, YHVH, is the greatness, the power, the glory, the victory and the majesty; for everything in heaven and on Earth is yours. The kingdom is yours, YHVH; and You are exalted as head over all* (I Chron. 29:11).**

1. **And why are they called *Sefirot?*** The discussion of the *Sefirot* is triggered by the priest holding up his ten fingers when he blesses the people (See §123-124).

2. **The heavens recount the Glory of God.** A wordplay. The word "recount," *m'SaPiRim,* contains the root *samech-payh-resh,* the same as *Sefirot.* The "Glory," or emanation of divinity, consists of ten forces. Being divine emanations themselves, words that are linguistically related also share in overlapping powers.

3. **They are three.** This suitably cryptic declaration that "ten are three" is drawing on *Sefer Yetzirah,* which teaches in yet another wordplay, "He created His universe with three books (*S'FaRim*): text (*Sefer*), number (*SeFaR*), and speech (*SiPuR*)" (1.1). The ten *Sefirot* are subsumed into three triads [plus the unique *Shekhinah*].

4. **Three hosts and three dominions.** Only two of the three triads are mentioned here, and only one of them, the "dominions," gets any further consideration. Like the *Sefirot* first expounded in *Sefer Yetzirah,* the *Bahir* offers no comprehensive study of the topic. Later works of Kabbalah will elaborate further on these triads, plus the *Shekhinah.*

5. **And light is the life of water.** An obscure phrase. It could be alluding to the order of creation in Gen. 1. The Talmud Bavli (*Chag.* 13a) holds that the study of creation, *ma'asei bereshit,* is an esoteric subject to be shared with only well-prepared students. Slight emendations of the phrase yields either "light of perfect life" or "light of the day of days." Neither is entirely satisfactory, so we keep the phrase as it appears in the received text.

6. **Holy beasts, the ofanim, the wheels of the chariot.** This refers to the revelation of the divine

Pleroma that appears in Ezekiel 1. The same Talmud passage that discusses *ma'asei bereshit* calls Ezekiel's vision the *ma'asei merkavah,* the lore of the divine chariot. This, too, is treated as an occult topic. The beasts, ofanim, and wheels are supernal entities that surround the image of God in Ezekiel's vision.

7. **Surrounded in holiness.** The word for holiness, *k'dushah,* has a double meaning: it means "holiness" in the abstract sense but is also the name of a prayer recited three times daily in Jewish liturgy. This is important to the rest of the teaching.

8. **The mystery of the great holy ones.** Based on the context, *Kedoshim* here refers to the angelic court which surrounds God, chants God's praises, and executes God's will.

9. **So they crown him with three 'holys.'** In Is. 6:6, the prophet Isaiah witnesses the angels shout "Holy! Holy! Holy!" in God's presence. This phrase becomes the centerpiece of the *k'dushah* prayer Jews recite. The mystical understanding is that "they" refers to both angels and men, who together "crown" God, i.e., affirm and sustain God's sovereignty. The prayer is an act of theurgy that allows God to exercise dominion over the universe. The Rabbis teach a similar notion of God's interdependence with humanity (MdRI *Pisha* 14; *PRK* 12:6). The other face of the "fearsome and awesome" God is explored in §131.

GEOFFREY W. DENNIS

HOW THE ONE ENTERS
THE WORLD OF MULTIPLICITY
§48(M); §32 (S-A)

It is written in one [verse], teaching,
And the people saw the voices (Ex. 20:15).
But it is written in another [verse],
They hear the sound of the words (Deut. 4:12).1
[This contradiction can be resolved]. How so?
At first, they were seeing voices. And what did
   they see?
Seven voices, as David said.2
But at the end, they heard the word going out
   from between them all.3
Wait, was this [not] ten, all of them speaking one
   word, of which the Rabbis spoke?4
Indeed, seven sayings of seven voices, but of the
   three [additional voices] it is written,5
**You heard the sound of the words, but you saw no
   image, only a voice** (Deut. 4:12). 6
Thus you learned they said all [ten] of them in
   one word,
In order that Israel would not err, saying,
"Others helped Him, or one from among the
   angels,
or that His voice alone was not powerful enough.
Thus, He repeated all of them [simultaneously]."7

RELATED BIBLICAL TEXT:

***Taste YHVH and see that he is good* (Ps. 34:8).**

1. **And the people saw the voices.** During the great theophany at Mount Sinai (Ex. 19-22). The first verse is describing the experience of synesthesia, of having one type of sensory experience through a different sensory organ (i.e., "tasting blue"). The second verse, by contrast, describes the more conventional idea of hearing the divine word. How can both be true?

2. Seven voices, as David said. In Psalm 29. The author has no doubt that the voice of God can be seen and does not even attempt to justify this oddity. But plural "voices?" This deserves comment. Ps. 29 reiterates the phrase "**voice of YHVH**" seven times. Many of the voices are described as having physical force. Jewish tradition concludes from this (*B.*, *Pes.* 112a; *Mid. The.* 2:68:6; *Tanchuma* Shemot 22; Yitro 6) that there were seven divine voices visible at Sinai. This also parallels the rabbinic claim that there are seven heavens, hierarchically arranged (*B. Chag.* 12b-13a).

3. **And at the end.** The visual voices each produced audible words, thus harmonizing the two verses.

4. **Wait, was this [not] ten?** A variant tradition to the "seven voices" is that God must make ten "descents/condensations" to engage with the material world, the 6th of which is to be present at Sinai, and the 7th to stand before Moses on top of the mountain (*Sifrei* Numbers 93; *MdRI* Yitro 3, 9; *PdRE* 14).

5. **Seven sayings.** The word written here for "saying," *amirin,* is wordplay on "treetops," associating the voices with the cosmic Tree of Life, the *Sefirot.* The wordplay repeats in line 12.

6. **You saw no image, only a voice.** In order to reconcile the two different traditions, those of the "seven"

and the "ten" means for God to become manifest in the world, a novel solution is put forward—the tradition speaks of "seven" because only seven were visible. In fact, there are ten, three of which are not available to human visual apprehension but can only be "heard."

7. He repeated all of them [simultaneously]. Lest people fall into the error of believing there were seven (or ten) different divinities addressing them at Sinai, all the potencies, together, uttered the singular word of the singular God. This teaching creates one conceptual umbrella; it establishes the entire basis for the centrality of the ten *Sefirot* in subsequent Jewish mysticism. It is saying, in effect, "even though the word '*Sefirot*' is not to be found in earlier Jewish metaphysics, in fact, the concept has always been there." The various rungs, heavens, voices, utterances, or descents of God mentioned in earlier sources are all really alluding to one phenomenon, the potencies of the *Sefirot*, which bridge the distance between the ineffable, unfathomable One and the manifold, manifest, and imperfect reality of our own experience.

MERCY AND JUSTICE:
THE RIGHT AND LEFT HAND OF GOD

WHEN THE HEBREW Bible speaks about God, the language is often archly anthropomorphic (God has a face, eyes, arms, hands, feet, a nose) and anthropopathic (God feels anger, pleasure, laughs). Yet the Bible also insists God has no form that can become seen or represented (Deut. 4:12; Ex. 20:3).

The Talmud resolves this conundrum by arguing that the Bible is applying metaphors to God, that "Scripture speaks in the language of men" (*Ber.* 31b), meaning it uses language that makes the incomprehensible comprehensible. In the 12th century, the Jewish philosopher Maimonides would devote the first chapter of his magnum opus, *Guide for the Perplexed*, to demonstrating that every single anthropomorphic reference to God in the Hebrew Bible was meant figuratively rather than literally. He accomplishes this by finding other verses in Scriptures where every human term applied to God—hand, arm, face, and leg—is used in a purely metaphoric fashion.

So the idea of God as pure spirit has deep roots in Jewish thought. Nonetheless, Jews have freely used "the language of men" to continue to describe divinity. So too here, the *Bahir* talks of God having two dimensions. Specifically, of having a "right" and "left" side. This expression is combined with the Rabbinic teaching that God has a conflicted personality, as it were; that God ever hovers between the divine attributes of Judgment and Compassion toward Creation (*Ber.* 7b; *Song of Songs R.,* XXXIV, 1-7). In one highly influential version of this, after failing to create universes based solely on one of these attributes, God comes to realize that the world must be a balance of both (*Gen. R.* 12:15).

While the Midrash occasionally invokes the idea that God has a right and left hand that serve as metonyms for these two attributes (*Sotah* 47b, *Song of Songs R.* 1:9.1), it is the *Bahir* that elevates this notion from a trope to an ideology. Henceforth, in kabbalistic literature, God is marked by a symmetry of polarities. The *Sefirot,* specifically, will be understood to be either "right-side" (*Chochmah, Chesed, Netzach*) or "left-side" (*Binah, Gevurah, Hod*) attributes, with balancing points to harmonize them (*Tiferet, Yesod, Malchut*). In time, the left side of God will become known as the *Sitra Achra,* the "other side," the side from which judgment, evil, and even the demonic emanates. But that is beyond the scope of the doctrines which appear in our texts.

Texts not included in this section but which have related content: §54(M); §36(S-A); §132(M); §90 (S-A) §156(M); §140(S-A).

GEOFFREY W. DENNIS

THE RIGHT AND LEFT HANDS OF GOD
§52(M); §34(S-A)

And for the one who has no silver,
Go to Him, because there is His 'silver.'
As it is written,
I have the silver and I have the gold (Hag. 2:8).1
What [does this mean] **I have the silver and I have the gold?**
A parable. To what may this be compared?
To a king who has two treasuries;
One of silver, one of gold.
That of silver is at his right. That of gold is at his left.
He said, "This [the silver] will be accessible and easy to take out."2
And he did gently, according to his word,
And he would cleave to the afflicted, and gently guide them.3
As it is written,
Your right hand, YHVH, noble in power . . . (Ex. 15:6).
And if one is content with his share, it is good,
And if not, the **right hand of YHVH will shatter the enemy** (Ex. 15:6).4
He said, this is the gold!4
As it is written, **I have the silver and I have the gold [declares YHVH of Hosts].**

RELATED BIBLICAL TEXT:

Long life is in her right hand; In her left hand are riches and honor (Prov. 3:16).

1. I have the silver and I have the gold. The speaker of this verse is YHVH. In its biblical context, this has a surprisingly literal meaning: God is the source of wealth. Here, this is taken to be figurative. "Silver" and "gold," like other mundane objects in the Bible, are redefined as symbolic of divine attributes or divine powers. In this case, they signify compassion and judgment.

2. This will be accessible and easy to take out. The king of the parable [God] prefers this to the alternative. The idea that God desires to be compassionate, rather than punishing, is a recurrent theme in both the Bible (Numbers 14:18) and the Talmud (*Ber.* 7b).

3. **And he would cleave to the afflicted, and gently guide them**. "Silver" is the divine attribute of love/kindness/charity.

4. **The right hand of YHVH will shatter the enemy.** If one is not content with gracious love, then one invites divine judgment. It also implies that what flows from God's good right hand can be misperceived as "shattering," as pure woe. A passage from Isaiah comes to mind: "Woe to those who call evil good and good evil (Is. 5:20)." Confusingly, the proof text refers twice to the "right hand" of God rather than, as the parable would have us expect, to the "left hand." This is in keeping with the deliberately mystifying nature of *Bahir*ic discourse, but perhaps the verse was chosen because it emphasizes that the two "treasuries" are in fact one. Somewhat subverting the parable, the proof-text emphasizes that such distinctions are fundamentally facile, that all flows ultimately from the same source, the "king."

5. He said, this is the gold! "Gold" is the divine attribute of judgment/severity. God has two sides, the loving, forgiving, merciful side, symbolized by "silver" and

"right hand," and the side of judgment, symbolized by "gold." Like humanity, God struggles to strike a balance between the two (*Lev. R.* 29.6). As the concept of the *Sefirot* further solidifies in the following centuries, kabbalistic texts regularly come to speak of the right and left side of the Godhead, with the right-side *sefirah* of *Chesed* being the potency of compassion, and left-side *Gevurah,* the potency of severe justice. In this way, the Kabbalists try to reconcile the existence of privation, suffering, and evil with their commitment to true monotheism.

GEOFFREY W. DENNIS

WINE AND MILK:
WISDOM WITHOUT LIMITS
§136-137(M); §93 (S-A)

What is loving-kindness?
It is Torah, as it is written,
All who are thirsty, come for water;1
Whoever does not have silver . . . (Is.55:1).2
This is 'silver,'
as it is written,
  **. . . come to Him, he who is without silver, and
without payment (Is. 55:1 cont.)3**
He will feed you Torah and teach you,
For you are already worthy through the merit of
  Abraham.
Who bestowed loving-kindness.4
Without silver, he would [provide] food and drink.
And [for one] without payment , in open loving-
  kindness,
[he would give] wine and milk.5
What is 'wine and milk?'
And what is the connection, one to the other?
To teach us that wine is fear and milk is love. 6

RELATED BIBLICAL TEXT:

*In that day the mountains will drip new wine,
and the hills will flow with milk; all the ravines of
Judah will burst forth with water. A fountain will
flow out of the house of YHVH and will water the
valley of acacias. (Joel 3:18).*

1. All who are thirsty, come for water. The beginning of a chain of associations. There is a long-standing homiletic connection in which "water" is understood to be a metaphor for "Torah" (*B. B.K. 82a; Ber. 61b; Gen. R. 54:1*).

2. Whoever does not have silver. Based on the parallelism of the verse, if water equals Torah, then silver equals Torah also.

3. And without payment. Giving without expecting payment is an act of *chesed,* "loving-kindness." Therefore, the correspondence is: Torah=water=silver=loving-kindness.

4. Who bestowed loving-kindness. Abraham is the personification of *chesed.* Because of that, the *sefirah* of *Chesed* will reciprocate on his descendants, even if they are not personally worthy of such love. It is a form of divine grace. The bestowal of grace is considered a uniquely Christian idea, but it has a significant place in Judaism also.

5. Wine and milk. This refers to two episodes in the life of Abraham. In Gen. 15, Abraham refuses to profit from his heroism in rescuing war captives and booty taken from the city of Sodom. Suddenly, a mysterious figure then appears, the priest Malchizedek, who honors him with a gift of wine and bread. In Gen. 18, he provides milk and a meal to anonymous wayfarers, who are later revealed to be angels bringing him the news that God is ending Sara's barrenness. In each case, an act of *chesed* is rewarded with a divine gift. Perhaps there is additional layer in that the wine, which is red, acknowledges the violence that undergirds the just act, while the milk is pure love, a symbol of motherly nurture.

6. Wine is fear and milk is love. Like water and silver, any commonplace object mentioned in the Torah is understood to an encoded symbol, a fingerpost pointing to a higher divine reality. Here, the two most potent aspects of God, the judgment we fear and the love we crave, are best when in homeostasis, one balanced against the other.

DIVINE SYZYGY:
THE MALE AND FEMALE SIDES OF GOD

ANOTHER MYTHIC FEATURE of *Sefer ha-Bahir* is that just as it oscillates between justice and mercy, the universe also operates on a principle of complementary male and female forces. This is an ancient pre-monotheistic idea, a belief that divinity is made of *syzygies*, "yoked" masculine and feminine principles. We moderns may actually relate to this concept better if we think of the almost abstract Taoist symbol of the Yin/Yang principle. You know the image—the black and white droplets that interlock, forming a complete circle, with the complementary tone appearing as a spot in the middle of each droplet. These symbolize universal male and female, active and passive forces, working in harmony. Around ancient Israel, these forces were usually expressed mythologically in tales of male gods and female consort goddesses who unite in a *hieros gamos*, a sacred marriage that animates the cosmos. [10] Gnosticism, a religious ideology of the Roman era, focused on the same concept in a less personified way, with the idea of male and female "emanations." It was the Gnostics who first used the word *syzygy* the way we are using it.

By contrast, the Hebrew Bible eschews this notion, abandoning all but a few vestigial mythological traditions about Divinity. Yet the idea that the Hebrew God has a female counterpart, a "consort," actually appears in a radically altered form in biblical and rabbinic thought. The Prophets and Sages both characterize the Jewish people as God's bride and wife. He is the "God of Israel" in the same way we would speak of the "husband of Joan." In rabbinic writings, this is often expressed as God's desire for the feminine *Knesset Yisrael*, "Assembly of Israel," a collective, idealized personification of the people. In monotheism, we call this "erotic theology." For the Israelite and later Jewish thinkers who affirm erotic theology, the most apt image for describing the intense, intimate relationship between God and the Jewish people is that of a man and woman. Not surprisingly, this theology mirrored the social assumptions of male/female relations found in traditional cultures—the male is the dominant, active partner who expects complete fidelity from his consort. The relationship is characterized as passionate but hardly egalitarian.

Sefer ha-Bahir continues the Jewish tradition of erotic theology while reintroducing and extending the older ideas of *syzygy* and *hieros gamos* but with a monotheistic twist. Not only does God have a relationship with Israel, now the One God's very being is made up of male and female aspects. The *Bahir* especially develops a lush vocabulary for the feminine aspect of God: Crown, Daughter, Footstool, Matron, Moon, Mother, Night, *Shekhinah*, Sister, Queen, Wisdom, and Princess, all of which are ultimately tropes for the feminine side of God. These figures, in turn, provide the *dramatis personae* for describing a dynamic celestial romance—God's male and female aspects become estranged when the creatures in creation fall into moral chaos. In turn, this estrangement fuels disharmony and imbalance in the Higher Realms. In time, kabbalistic writings will aggregate these many grades of the divine feminine into one overarching entity, the *Shekhinah*. But in the *Bahir*, the feminine forces in the Godhead are more varied and elusive.[11]

The very large number of teachings on this subject

provided below testifies to the centrality of this idea to Kabbalah. In subsequent centuries, the topic of divine syzygy never loses its hold of the mystical imagination, making this one of the *Bahir*'s great contributions to medieval Jewish thought.

Texts not included in this section but which have related content: §3(M); §3 (S-A); §27(M); §19 (S-A) 27/19; §83(M); §56 (S-A).

DIVINE ANDROGYNY
§198-199(M); §140 (S-A)

The Holy One of blessing created man male and female,1

As it is written, **male and female He created them** (Gen. 1:27).

[So how] is it possible to say this?2

See, it is written, **God created the man in his image, in the image of God He created him** (Gen. 1:26).3

Then, only afterward, **I will make him a helper beside him** (Gen. 2:18).

Then He took one side of him and enclosed flesh around it (Gen. 2:21).4

Rather, I observe it is written concerning them,

He *formed*, it is written, He *made*, and it is written He *created*.5

At the time **He made** the soul (1:26).

He created them; male and female (1:27).

He formed (Gen. 2:7) at the time the soul was mounted upon the body, when He added the spirit.

And how do we know "formed" means "assembled?"

As it is written, **YHVH God assembled all the beasts of the field and the birds of air from the earth6**

and He brought each to the man to see what to name it (Gen. 2:19).

And it was [later] written, **Male and female he created them** (Gen. 5:2),

and it is written, **then He blessed them** (Gen. 5:24).

1. **Created man male and female.** The first human, *adam,* was androgynous. Much in what follows hinges on the word *adam,* which simultaneously means the first human and "man/humanity." The actual word that appears in the Genesis narrative is not, as is commonly translated, "Adam," a proper name. Rather Genesis repeatedly calls him *ha-adam,* "the man," or more literately, "the earthling," since he was derived from the earth.

2. He created them. Since verse 27 clearly makes the object of God's creation "them" (more than one being), how is the claim that God created one androgynous being plausible?

3. **In the image of God He created him.** The verse preceding 27 describes God making only a single being, a being made in the divine image, and one without a body, like God. Thus the division into male and female only comes after the initial act of creating humanity. The next proof text, 2:2, confirms this interpretation. This is a variation on an ancient claim, repeated throughout rabbinic literature (*B. Ber*.61a; *Yev.* 63b; *Gen. R.* 8:1; 17:2), that man was initially a single creature, containing both male and female attributes. This belief was shared by some ancient Gnostics (*On the Origin of the World; Poimandres* I.12).

4. **Then He took one side of him.** Most translations render *mitzalotav* as "from his rib." But *tzeila* can also mean "side." (Ex. 25:12, 14; 27:7; 37:3,5). God is understood to sever the feminine side of *adam* the androgyne from the male side.

5. **He *formed*, it is written, He *made*, and it is written He *created*.** The Torah uses three different verbs applied to the creation of humanity, *yatzar, asah,*

The soul of the male is from the masculine [side]
And the soul of the female is from the feminine
  [side]. 7

RELATED RABBINIC TEXT:

**Any man who does not have a woman is not a
human being (B., Yev. 63a).**

and *bara*. What follows is a demonstration that each signifies a different stage of a protracted process. This model would influence the later *Pardes Rimmonim*, which expounded the paradigm of the "four worlds of emanation."

6. God assembled all the beasts of the field and the birds of air from the earth. Again, the author appeals to a less conventional use of a word. *Yatzar* usually means to "form," but also means "assemble/gather." So using this sense of the word, God *yatzar,* "assembled" the new human by adding a body to the soul, the implication being that *adam* in its first iteration was both androgynous and purely spiritual. The body only followed the decision to divide humanity into separate male and female entities.

7. The soul of the female is from the feminine [side]. All women are formed from the feminine aspect of the human soul, all men from the masculine aspect. Thus, no one person of either gender possesses a single human soul, only the fragment of one. Companionship and marriage is therefore an act of cosmic significance; of reuniting the polarities, of becoming more wholly human, and godly, as God first intended. The unstated corollary of this is that God is androgynous, containing both male and female aspects. This is the "image of God" we shared with God at the beginning—being one, being bi-gendered, and being incorporeal.

Geoffrey W. Dennis

The Splendor of All
§173(M); §117 (S-A)

What is 'splendor?' 1
It is the splendor of all. 2
And splendid is the Song of Songs,
concerning it, it is written,3
Who is this that shines as the dawn,
beautiful as the moon,
radiant as the sun,
awesome as the stars in their courses? (Song of
  Song 6:10).
And it is splendid because of the female;4
For that reason the female was taken from the
  man,
Because it is not possible for the world below
to exist without the female.5

Related Biblical Text:

You have made him little less than divine;
adorned him in glory and splendor (Ps. 8:6)

1. What is 'splendor?' The Hebrew word *hadar*. This word's meaning is manifold in the Hebrew Bible, being translated as "majesty," "honor," "glory," "beautiful," "ornament," "splendor," and "array." This translation opts for "splendid" because it is of the rhetoric of the proof text (Song of Songs 6:10) describing this fundamental divine attribute, but any of these semantically rich meanings could be substituted, giving this teaching a kaleidoscopic quality.

2. It is the splendor of all. It is the divine essence that imbues all things, granting all things supernal meaning and sublime value.

Concerning it, it is written. Concerning the 'splendor.' Since rabbinic times, the Song of Songs is understood to be an allegory, a parabolic account of the passionate love between God and the people Israel (*Shir ha-Shirim R.*), God and the soul (*Commentary of Issak ibn Sahula*), God and the mind (*Commentary of Gersonides*), or between the male and female attributes of God (*Commentary of Ezra of Gerona*). Regardless, this description is understood to apply to the feminine divine potency, as the verse in question, 6:10, refers to the female lover.

3. Because of the female. This most awesome attribute is finally explicitly called the female attribute, the life-giving or generative aspect of God.

4. It is not possible for the world below to exist. The splendid array, the glorious multiplicity of our cosmos, is made possible and sustained solely because of *hadar*. While it remains embedded in singularity, its potential remains unrealized; only when it emanates from the divine essence or, on the human dimension, when it is detached from the male, does it reveal its role and, with it, its splendor.

THE PARABLE OF THE DESIRABLE GEM
§72(M); §49(S-A)

Another interpretation [of] **YHVH, enliven your actions in the midst of the years** (Hab. 3:2).
A parable. To what can this be compared?
To a king who has a beautiful jewel,
And she is the [most] desirable [feature] of his kingdom.1
At the time of his enjoyment, he embraces her, and kisses her,2
And places her on his head, and loves her.3
Habakkuk would say to Him: Even [though] the angels are with You,4
This jewel is the most desirable of Your cosmos; 5
Therefore, **enliven your actions in the midst of the years.**
What is the meaning of the expression, 'years?'
As it is written, **And God said, let there be light, and there was light** (Gen. 1:5).
And 'light' means nothing other than 'day,' as it is written,
And the great light governed the day, while the lesser light governed the night (Gen. 1:15).6
And [since] years consist of days, so it is written,
enliven your actions in the midst of the years.
It is the jewel that gives birth to the years.7

Related Biblical Text:

How beautiful are your feet in sandals, O prince's daughter! Your rounded thighs are like jewels, the work of a master hand. (Song of Songs 7:1).

1. **the [most] desirable**. The Hebrew word *chemdat* means both "precious" and "desirable." To appreciate the double-game being played, the latter is the better translation. Is the "jewel" really a royal ornament, something else, or both simultaneously?

2. **At the time of his enjoyment.** Again, a double-entendre. *Simchah* can mean "joy" and "aroused." The situation is discernibly sexual. The parable is simultaneously evasive and coyly erotic about its intended topic.

3. **And places her on his head**. The culminating act of what appears to be a sexual trajectory of behaviors. Or then again, sometimes a jewel is only a jewel. Perhaps this object really is a crown, and this is meant to describe God embracing the attribute of sovereignty.

4. **Habakkuk would say to Him.** The prophet seemingly breaks the fourth wall of this allegory. Is the parable now over, since the prophet is speaking of angels (or "kings" in some manuscripts), or is he now part of the parable, for he continues to use the parabolic and objectifying rhetoric of a "jewel" when a female supernal force is the actual subject? Regardless, this entity rivals the rest of the divine *Pleroma*, combined.

5. **This jewel is the most desirable of Your cosmos.** Translated here as "cosmos," *olam* can have both a spatial and temporal meaning, "space-time." Here, the connotation of "time" is emphasized. What makes the "jewel" so desirable, and what does the *hieros gamos* suggestively woven into the parable achieve? A seemingly tangential bit of textual analysis will lead to the answer.

6. **The lesser light governed the night.** We should note the inclusion of "night" when the first clause

concerning the day is sufficient to prove the point the author is making. The merism of "day" and "night" compliments the description of the divine syzygy of male and female merged into one; moreover, this alludes to the concept of divine androgyny, as a full "day" consists of both light and darkness.

7. **It is the jewel that gives birth to the years**. It is the supernal union of male and female forces in the divine *Pleroma* that creates time and history, existence as we know it. In the later development of Kabbalah, the "jewel" here will become identified as the *sefirah* of *Binah,* the "higher" female force from which creation emanates. This author of this teaching offers a metaphysical intuition but does not, or cannot, speak with more specificity.

GEOFFREY W. DENNIS

THE PARABLE OF THE HIDDEN BRIDE
§156(M); §104 (S-A)

And what is the meaning of, **[I bring seed from the east] and from the west I gather you** (Is. 43:5)?

From the attribute that always inclines toward the west.1

And why is it [the west] called *ma'arev*?

Because all the seed is mingled [*mitarev*] there.2

To what is this to be compared?

To a king ['s son] who had a lovely and chaste bride hidden in his chamber.3

He would take riches from his father's house and bring them to her.

She, in turn, would take everything, hide it, and mingle it together.

In time, he wanted to see what he had gathered and accumulated,

Therefore it is written, **and from the west I will gather you.**

And what is his father's house?

That which is written [preceding it], **I bring seed from the east.**4

This teaches us that it is brought from the east and sowed in the west.5

Then He gathers what He has sown. 6

RELATED BIBLICAL TEXT:

The Mighty One, God, Adonai, speaks and summons the earth from the rising of the sun to where it sets. From Zion, perfect in beauty, God shines forth (Ps. 50:1-2).

1. **The attribute that always inclines toward the west**. Unlike the ambiguity of the *Parable of the Gem,* this is clearly referring to the feminine aspect of divinity, elsewhere called the *Shekhinah.* This is probably based on the claims of Rabbi Akiba and Rabbi Joshua ben Levi that the "the *Shekhinah* is [or favors] in the west" (*B. B. B.* 25a). This association of the Divine feminine with the west continues in Midrash (*Tanchuma,* Buber, Shemot 10). The land of Israel, the proper dwelling place of the divine presence, is often referred to as "the west" in the Talmud.

2. **Because all the seed is mingled there**. The male [i.e., the "seed" from the east] and female divine polarities that interact with the lower worlds are harmonized in the Land of Israel, which is what makes that particular spot on Earth the "Holy Land."

3. **Hidden in his chamber.** Here, the chamber signifies the Temple in Jerusalem, the dwelling place of the divine presence (Ps. 50:1-2). As in other parables in the *Bahir,* there is a [deliberate?] ambiguity as to one of the parabolic figures. The text literally says "king"—who would, in traditional rabbinic parables, be God—but then mentions "his father's house." Who would be God's father? This commentary takes this parable to be describing the interactions of two *Sefirot* and therefore reads "king" as an ellipsis for the "king's son," i.e., the masculine attribute of God.

4. **I bring seed from the east**. The male divine attribute. In later Kabbalah, this is either *Tiferet* or *Yesod* on the *Sefirotic* tree of life, or is called *ha-Kadosh Baruch Hu,* "The Holy One, Blessed be He." This is an unusual parable for *Bahir,* not for its contents but for the fact that it actually includes a *nimshal,* an explanatory conclusion, vague as it may be.

5. **It is brought from the east and sowed in the west.** This begins the brief *nimshal*. It is arguing that Isaiah's use of "east" and "west" has an esoteric meaning. He is not only referring to the cardinal directions but is deploying them as a *merism*, two extreme points that encompass a totality, like "night and day," "good and evil," or "heaven and Earth." In this case, the male ["east," "seed," and "semen"] and female ["west," "chamber," and "sown"] potencies.

6. **Then He gathers what He has sown.** This is referring to the Godhead causing the continuing fructification and expansion of life in the world through the *hieros gamos*, or alternatively, it may be forward looking to the messianic era, or the final redemption of the world. Perhaps it meant to allude to both.

GEOFFREY W. DENNIS

THE PARABLE OF THE PLEASANT WIFE
§76(M only)

> ... **And God** saw the children of Israel, and God **knew** (Ex. 2:25).
> What is the meaning of, **and God knew?**1
> A parable. **To** what can this be compared?2
> A king had a pleasant wife, and had children from her.
> He embraced them and raised them, but they went off to evil ways.
> He then hated them and he hated her.
> Their mother turned to them and said, "My children! Why are you doing this?
> Your father hates both you and me!"
> [She continued] until they repented and returned to doing the will of their father.
> When their father saw this, he loved them as in the beginning.
> He then remembered their mother.3
> This is the meaning of
> **God saw the** children of Israel and God knew.
> So too it is written,
> **In the midst** of years, make them known.4

RELATED BIBLICAL TEXT:

Listen, my son, to your father's instruction and do not forsake your mother's teaching. They are a garland to grace your head and a chain to adorn your neck (Prov. 1:8-9).

1. **God** **knew.** The verb *v'yeda* means "know/understand," but also "have sexual intercourse." The author rhetorically wonders what the verse is trying to reveal. He believes the divine *Pleroma* is divided into male and female potencies, which together form a complementary whole. Like the two horses pulling a chariot, for these potencies to properly drive the created universe, they must be in harmony with each other.

2. A parable. Here, the author does not even explicitly state the principle to be explained as a Talmudic sage would. Before launching into the analogy, the rhetorical question is enough of a clue for the enlightened, emphasizing that this is not a teaching meant to be openly expounded for a mass audience.

3. He remembered their mother. The *nimshal*, the explanation normally offered at the end of a rabbinic parable, is also left unstated, once again highlighting the esoteric nature of this teaching. But the essence of the thing is this: the king is the male aspect of Divinity. The wife is the feminine dimension of the Godhead; perhaps she is personified Wisdom. She is calling the people to return (Pro. 1:2). When the children [of Israel] listen to her and obey God's will, the male potency of divinity "remembers" the female, they "know" one another (are reunited), and the harmony of the cosmos undergoes a restoration. In other words—and this is the shocking reversal of the power relationship between God and humanity that must be reserved for the wise—the ultimate harmony of the higher worlds actually depends on the human response.

4. Make them known. Bring the divine emanations of the male and female into confluence with each other. "Years" signals the mingling of days and nights, another syzygistic pairing. The Habakkuk passage, unstated in the

Bahir, continues, " . . . **though angry, You may remember love,"** reinforcing the meaning of the parable.

GEOFFREY W. DENNIS

THE HIDDEN FACE OF GOD (PART 1)
§130-131(M); §90 (S-A)

Praised be the Glory of YHVH from its place (Ezek. 3:12).
And what is the Glory of YHVH?[1]
A parable: it may be compared to a king
who had a noble woman in his chamber,[2]
and all his retinue were comforted by her.[3]
She had sons, and they would come every day
Into the presence of the king and bless him.
And they would say, "Where is our mother?"[4]
He would answer, "You are not able to see her now."
And they would respond, "Well, blessed is she,
Wherever she is."[5]

RELATED BIBLICAL TEXT:

It has been concealed from the sight of every living creature and hidden even from the birds in the skies (Job 28:21).

1. The Glory of YHVH. The divine Glory (*Kavod*) is mentioned many times in the Hebrew Bible. It is an apprehensible manifestation of God, what is visible to humanity when God is revealed to them. Often, it is a kind of nimbus or aureole that simultaneously reveals and conceals God's presence on Earth. In some passages, most notably Ezek. 1, it has anthropomorphic features.

2. A noble woman in his chamber. This noble woman (literally, *matronita,* borrowed from the Latin for "high lady" or "mistress"). In this context, it could also mean "queen." This teaching is quite distinct from §130-131, where the children have access to their mother. While the image of a woman cloistered by a controlling man is distinctly medieval, the purpose of the analogy is to teach that this feminine potency dwells within the very essence of God. The word for chamber, *heder,* simultaneously means "chamber," "secret [place]," and "womb."

3. Were comforted by her. Or "were consoled." She commands affection, apparently in a way the king does not, and so is essential to the king and his kingdom.

4. And they would say, "Where is our mother?" The sons are humanity, most likely the people Israel. They yearn for the presence of God to be more evident in their daily lives.

5. Wherever she is. Jews in their daily prayers bless God daily but also pray, *Baruch Kavod Adonai, mi'm'komo,* "Blessed be the Glory of God, from its place." This poignant parable invokes the pathos of the separation from the intimate experience of God, which many people crave in their day-to-day lives. As is often the case in the *Bahir,* no *nimshal,* no ready-made interpretation, is offered. But we can offer our own: God is inscrutable and, from our perspective, God's absence is inexplicable, but we can draw

comfort from the knowledge that the Glory still resides someplace and the possibility of luminous encounter still exists.

GEOFFREY W. DENNIS

THE EXILED FACE OF GOD (PART 2)
§132(M); 90(S-A)

And why is it written, **from its place** (Ezek. 3:12)?
That nobody knows its place.1
A parable: A daughter of a king
Came from far away and no one knew2
from whence she came,
until they saw she was a valorous woman,
pleasant and competent in all her actions,3
and they said, "This one is taken from the side of
  light,4
for all her deeds illuminate the world."
They asked her, "Where do you come from?"
She [would only] say, "From my place."5
They answered, "Well, if so, then great are the
  people of your place."6
"Blessed be she, and blessed be her place."

RELATED BIBLICAL TEXT:

*You are the place where we can find refuge. (Jer.
17:12).*

1. **Nobody knows its place.** The hermeneutic occasion is the odd biblical expression: **Praised be the Glory of YHVH from its place** (Ezek. 3:12). The location of God's Glory is indeterminate. When the Temple stood, the Shekhinah/Glory was widely understood to dwell there, in the midst of the people.

2. **Came from far away.** This parable alludes to two well-known rabbinic teachings. One that explained that from the time of the expulsion from Eden, for seven generations, the Shekhinah withdrew from the world (*Gen. R.* 19:7), and the other, that the Shekhinah did not withdraw again when the Temple was destroyed but instead accompanied the people into exile (*B. d Meg.* 29a; *R. H.* 3a; *B. Ḳ.* 25a).

3. **Pleasant and competent in all her actions.** This is a striking, active image of a woman. This is also an unusually affectionate and quaint parable. Rather than being about kings and queens, it centers on a virtuous woman, but not a noble woman, and villagers gossiping about a stranger.

4. **This one is taken from the side of light**. She is a manifestation of God's right hand, or right side, the attribute of compassion.

5. **She [would only] say.** This element of the parable explains the expression **from its place** but begs the question: is God's presence merely being coy, or has it, in its exile, forgotten its source entirely? If it is the latter, this adds an even greater level of mystery and drama, drawing to reader into sympathy with the damaged (a divine amnesiac, as it were) fractured deity.

6. **Then great are the people of your place.** You come from good stock. Yet if the parabolic meaning of the "place"

is God, then the reference to "people" seems an odd addition. Is this an allusion to the *Pleroma*, the fullness of the divine order? In the earlier teaching, the divine Glory is hidden from her children. Here, by contrast, she is with her children but hidden from her divine consort. The concluding line invokes a blessing on the feminine and masculine ("her place") sides of divinity, with the implicit hope that when reunited, the unified God will further "illuminate the world."

PARABLE OF THE KING'S CHAMBERS
§63(M); §43(S-A)

What is His heart?
He said, "If this is the case [you don't already
  know], Ben Zoma is outside, and you are with
  him."1
"Heart" stands for the concealed thirty-two, and
  through them, the world was created.
And what are the thirty-two?
He said to them, the thirty-two paths.2
A parable: a king was in his inner-most chamber.3
The number of chambers [in his palace] is thirty-
  two.
And each chamber has its own path.
Is it fitting for the king to invite all into his
  chambers by these paths? You would say, no.
Is it fitting for him to expose his pearls, treasures,
  gems, and jewels? No.
So what did he do?
He touched his daughter, and concealed all the
  paths in her
And within her garments.4
So whosoever desires to enter must gaze into
  [her] face.
Then he married her to a king. Moreover, she was
  given to him as a gift.5
And sometimes, in his love, he calls her "lover,"
because they came from a place where they were
  one.6
But sometimes he calls her "my daughter,"
  because she is his daughter.
And sometimes he calls her "mother."7

1. **And you are with him.** A student is posing a question springing from an earlier teaching regarding the "heart of God." The teacher considers this question so elementary that he responds sarcastically with an allusion to Ben Zoma, a sage who pursued esoteric wisdom but proved unable to grasp what he learned and went mad (*B. Chag.* 14b). The teacher is saying, "If this is not known to you already, you are not ready to learn more." Nevertheless, he continues but couches the lesson in a (supposedly) easy-to-grasp parable.

2. **The thirty-two paths.** The thirty-two paths of wisdom described in *Sefer Yetzirah,* a foundational text of Jewish number-word mysticism. Evidently, the students have failed to study it. The "thirty-two" refers to the 22 letters of the Hebrew *alef-bet* and the numbers 1-10, the *Sefirot.* According to *Sefer Yetzirah,* these are the building blocks, the supernal periodic table, as it were, which God uses to construct the cosmos.

3. **A parable.** This seems inspired by an already daring erotic parable found in *Song of Songs R.* 3:11, where God takes Israel, his "daughter," as His lover and, in the end, calls the people "mother" (i.e., once united, God and the people give birth to some unspecified thing).

4. **He touched his daughter**. Up to this point, the rhetoric of hidden chambers and treasures, and the paths to them, has had an erotic subtext that now bursts to the surface with the "touch." But what or who is the daughter? I propose, contra other interpreters who claim she is Israel or the *Sefirot,* that she is meant to stand for Wisdom/Torah. All of God's secret wisdom, and the pathways to that wisdom, is concealed in the esoteric meanings of Torah and its "garments" (i.e., its attractive "outer" trappings: narratives, genealogies, poems, etc.).

And I saw that you were ready for love (Ezek. 16:8)

5. **Then he married her to a king.** The meaning of this pivotal sentence is much disputed. Based on the earlier parable in *S. of S. R.* 3.11, some propose the transgressive-erotic idea that the king marries his own daughter. Yet the sentence is transitive; there is apparently a third party. One piquant proposal is that a previously unnamed "he" (either a higher aspect of God or a higher *sefirah*, thus making the king and his daughter lower male and female forces in the godhead who serve the divine essence) unites the two. This fits well with the later, more elaborate structured models of the *Sefirot* to be found in the *Zohar* and beyond. Alternately, the king gives his daughter to a third party, a groom/king, which I would take to be the people Israel. Thus Torah and Israel are wed. This also follows a pattern in both earlier rabbinic writings and other contemporaneous parables, such as *Tanchuma*, Pekude 4. The writer must leave it to the reader to choose, but this commentary continues following the third premise.

6. **They came from a place where they were one**. Erotic union aside, Torah and Israel are already ontologically related, "sister and brother," emanations of the one God. Much later mystics, like Moses Luzatto, will articulate this as a quasi-doctrine: "God, Torah, and Israel are one."

7. **Sometimes.** Assuming the parable is discussing God (the king), Torah (the daughter), and Israel (the groom/king), then the unstated *nimshal* is as follows: the heart of God is found in the words and numbers of Torah. God *and* Israel engage with Torah in a *gamos hieros,* a sacred union that pleases and strengthens God; Torah is Israel's "daughter" in the sense that Israel has authority over it (see §3); the Torah is the "mother" of new insights and teachings that revitalize the godhead and give birth to a better world.

THE PARABLE OF
THE GLORIOUS DAUGHTER
§54(M); §36(S-A)

What is its function here?1
A parable: To what may it be compared?
To a king who had a goodly, pleasant, comely, and
  perfect daughter.
So he married her to a prince.
He dressed her, crowned her, he adorned her,
And gave her great wealth.
But, is it possible for the king to [entirely] let her
  leave his palace?
You would [have to] say, "no."
Is it possible for him to dwell with her constantly?
You would [have to] say, "no."
What must he do?
There is a window between them,
And at any hour that the daughter needs her
  father,
Or the father needs his daughter,
They unite by way of the window.2
Thus it is written, **The king's daughter is glorious
  within her chamber;**
**Her gown is interwoven gold [and she is brought
  inside to the king]** (Ps. 45:13-14)3

1. Its function? This continues an earlier discussion, in §53, but also shares the theme of God sharing his divine consort with a "prince" (humanity, or Israel) found in §63. What is the function of the *bet* in the word *zahav,* "gold," which, we have learned in §53, symbolizes the *hieros gamos* that drives creation? How does the *bet* facilitate the union of the *Sefirotic* male and female described there?

2. They unite by way of the window. A wild and provocative erotic parable. The masculine and feminine attributes are separated and reunited. God has given His female potency (the "daughter"), probably meant to be understood as the Glory or Torah, to humanity or the people Israel (the "prince"). Yet God cannot sustain the cosmos without a female side, so there must be an avenue for God to perform the necessary *hieros gamos* as needed. The shape of the *bet,* which is enclosed on three sides but has a "window" on the fourth, hints at this cosmic passageway between the upper and lower realms that allows this female energy to sustain both.

3. Her gown is interwoven gold. This proof text buttresses the metaphor of the parable, and the language of the verse highlights how "gold" is the symbolic code-word of divine syzygy, it being "interwoven." The special message of this passage is that the "daughter" (Torah, the Glory, or perhaps, though less likely, *Shekhinah*) not only fructifies the cosmos but actually mediates between God and the world.

Related Biblical Text:

Take me with you; come, let's run! The king has brought me into his bedroom. Young Women of Jerusalem How happy we are for you, O king. We extol your love even more than wine. How right they are to adore you. (Song of Songs 1:4).

Cosmic Correspondence:
As Above, So Below

J UST AS THE *Bahir* is preoccupied with "horizontal" polarities (right and left; male and female) in need of harmonization, so too it understands the totality of being as based on a "vertical" merism: Heaven and Earth. But in this regard, the perception is different. More than a dichotomy, the Bahir believes in a correspondence between the world order and the heavenly order. This is not original to the *Bahir* but grows out of the Platonic notion of the paired concept of Macrocosm and Microcosm; that there is a cognate similarity in pattern, nature, or structure between human beings and the universe.

The Jewish concept of heaven and Earth mirroring each other is broader than simply that humanity is a microcosmic reflection of the universe. This sense of what is below reflects what is above is applied to many entities, a concept that draws on another Platonic concept, the doctrine of forms; that there exist in the realm of ideas myriad ideal versions of everything that exists on Earth. So, for example, while we have many, many forms of chairs here on Earth, they all emanate from the "ideal form" of the concept "chair" that exists on high.

The specifically Jewish version of this, while likely having its roots in Greek philosophy, has a distinctive beginning in the concept of central Jewish institutions (Jerusalem) having their ideal counterpart in the heavens (*Yerushalyim shel maalah,* "Jerusalem on High"). The same applies to entities such as the Temple, the priesthood, and the Torah.

The exact place where this idea emerges in Jewish thinking is unclear, though evidence points to priestly spirituality in the centuries before the Common Era (AD/CE). In the Dead Sea Scrolls, there is a belief that harmony between the worlds depends on the harmonious actions of earthly priests with their angelic counterparts who serve in the metaphysical Temple. The angels even have a high priestly angel (either Michael or Metatron) that parallels the earthly high priest. Later, the idea enters into the broader Jewish imagination. Thus, in the Talmud, we see the Sages find a proof-text for this idea, Psalms 122:3, "Jerusalem built up, a city knit together," and see it implied by Ezekiel 28:14, 16-17.

But this notion gets a broader application in the notion of the human microcosm (Heb. *Olam katan*). Gen. 1:27 informs us we are "made in the image of God," of course, but the Sages find further proof in Job, where he declares, "In my flesh, I see God" (19:26).

In the Talmud, we also encounter the concept of the ideal or primordial man (*Adam Ilyon, Adam Kadmon*) who is in fact co-equal with the universe (Deut. 4:32; *B. B. B.* 58a; *Pesikta de Rav Kahana* 4:4, 12:1, *Lev. R.* 20:2). All earthly humans, in all our diversity (Gen. 1-11), are in his ideal image (*B. B.B.*58a).

The importance of this is that makes human beings the nexus point between worlds and potential conduits of divine knowledge, blessing, and power. The *Bahir* takes this idea of an anthropomorphic universe and begins to reconcile it with the more abstract model of the *Sefirot*. In later centuries, the *Sefirotic* tree of life will even be superimposed on the image of Adam Kadmon, creating a doctrine of divine emanations that strives to be simultaneously anthropocentric and aniconic.

The teachings that appear in this section [and in other sections as well] are attempts to tease out the specifics of this relationship.

Texts not included in this section but which have related content: §196(M); §137(S-A); §198-199(M); §140(S-A).

GEOFFREY W. DENNIS

ORDER FROM CHAOS,
CHAOS WITHIN ORDER
§11-12(M); §9 (S-A)

And what does it mean,
The one no less than the other was God's doing
(Eccl. 7:14)?
He created *bohu* and placed it within peace.
He created *tohu* and placed it within woe.1
Bohu is within peace, as it is written, **He makes
peace in his high places** (Job 25:2).
This teaches that Michael, the Prince at the right
of the Holy One of blessing,
is water and hail,
while Gabriel, the Prince at the left of the Holy
One of blessing, is fire,2
and the Peaceable Ruler harmonizing between
them.3
This is [the meaning] of what is written, **He
makes peace in his high places.**4
So how do we know that *tohu* is within woe?
As it is written, **He forms peace and creates woe**
(Is. 45:7).
In this respect woe is from *tohu* and peace is from
*bohu.*5

RELATED BIBLICAL TEXT:

***Produce what is noble out of the worthless, and
you will be like My mouth* (Jer. 15:19).**

1. He created *bohu* . . . within peace . . . *tohu* . . . within woe. *Tohu* (desolation) and *bohu* (chaos), along with water, are the primordial substances from which God forms the cosmos. In the new order, these become aspects of *shalom* (peace, wholeness) and *ra* (woe, evil).

2. Michael . . . is water and hail; Gabriel . . . is fire. These princely angels personify two chaotic and polarized forces, fire and water. (*Deut. R.* 5:12). In western esoteric tradition, the angels and their qualities are reversed, with Michael being fire and Gabriel water.

3. **The Peaceable Ruler.** A title for God, derived from Is. 9:5: **Eternal Father, a peaceable ruler.**

4. **He makes peace in his high places.** God is able to tame contradictory elementary forces and transform them for the good. While fire and water retain their primeval capacity for chaos, they are also essential beneficent elements in the new cosmos.

5. **In this respect woe is from *tohu* and peace is from *bohu*.** By reversing the claim, it is emphasized that desolation and chaos are not absent from the world, only curbed. The divine drama of building and transformation continues; God's creation is still rife with contradictions and conflicts. But we, made in the divine image, may imitate God in reconciling these forces for the good.

THE UNIVERSAL BEING
§82(M); §55(S-A)

And what are the seven limbs in a human being?1
It is written, **In the image of God He made the human** (Gen. 7:6).
It is further written, **Because in the image of God He created** him (Gen. 1:27).
[The image resides] in all his limbs and all his parts.2
And what have we said, in what way does the *vav* resemble [the verse]
Wrapped in light like a garment (Ps. 104:2)?
What is vav? It is none other than the six directions.3
He said, "*Brit Milah* and its [female] counterpart of the man is considered one,4
the two hands [make] three, his head and torso [make] five, and his two legs [make] seven.5
The powers of heaven are analogous, as is written, **God made this equal to that** (Eccl. 7:14).
These are [also] the [seven] days, as is written,
Because the YHVH made six days, the heaven, and the earth (Ex. 31:17).
It doesn't read "*In* six days," in order to teach that each day has its own power.6

RELATED BIBLICAL TEXT:

***God created man on Earth from one end of the heavens to the other; has anything as grand as this ever happened, or has its equal even been known?* (Deut. 32:4)**

1. What are the seven limbs? The passage prior to this refers to *zayin*/seven as emblematic of the human body. Now, we are going to have the seven limbs enumerated and learn about how these serve as cosmic signifiers.

2. All his parts. Seven key body parts correspond to the seven *hechalot*, the seven supernal palaces, which constitute the divine *Pleroma*. Thus "in the divine image" means every human bears the image of the divine order.

3. **The six directions.** This defies the *zayin*/seven that has been the hermeneutic principle until this point, a classic moment of obfuscating *Bahir*ic rhetoric. The numeric value of the Hebrew letter *vav* is six. In this case, the heavens, God's garment, extend to the four compass points, the zenith, and the nadir.

4. Counterpart of the man. *Brit Milah* is the rite of circumcision, here used as a euphemism for the penis. The genitalia of men and women are the chief morphological difference this interpretation feels the need to highlight. Concerning the other six points of resemblance, this applies equally to both men and women.

5. Makes seven. Note that the resemblance between God and humanity is found in shared numbers as well as in "shapes." The same applies to the human body's resemblance to divinity.

6. The YHVH made six days. The *Bahir* finally reveals how the numbers six and seven complement, rather than contradict, one another. This shares with §157-158(M); §104 (S-A) the conceit that the days of the week are entities of power, corresponding to the seven palaces and the seven "parts" of the human being. Six of these are ordinary, but the seventh is key to all. The Day of Rest, the seventh day, though not mentioned explicitly, is unique. It corresponds

to the male/female limb, which was counted as "one." It is the harmonizing catalyst for the male/female antipodes in divinity. Each person is a microcosm of the godhead on a spatial, temporal, and creative level. Shabbat is the day that most resembles the Godhead in perfect harmony. Therefore, human participation in this harmonizing principle, the Day of Rest, is not only a taste of perfect communion between God and humanity, it most fully activates the divine image that lies within us all.

GEOFFREY W. DENNIS

THE REVELATION OF THE EAR
(Part 1—*Alef*) §79 (M)/ §53 (S-A)

He [Habakkuk] understood the thought of the
  Holy One of blessing.
 Just as thought has no end—1
for man's thinking never reach the end, even unto
  eternity—
so too, the ear has no end, or to [its] hearing.2
As it is written, **The ear cannot have enough of
  hearing** (Eccl. 1:8).
And what is the reason?
Because the ear is the image of *alef*,3
And the *alef* is the essence of the Ten
  Commandments,
Therefore, **the ear cannot have enough of hearing.**
  5

RELATED BIBLICAL TEXT:

**How precious also are Your thoughts to me, O
God! What is the essence of their beginning? (Ps.
139:17)**

1. **Just as thought has no end.** See Isaiah 40:28.

2. The ear has no end. The ear represents the divine mind. This teaching takes us from the general idea of correspondence between the human being and the cosmos and focuses on this one specific human structure/sense. The role of hearing occupies a unique role in the Jewish understanding of the divine-human relationship. Humanity is more likely to "hear" divine revelation than to see it (Gen. 3:8; Deut. 6:4; 32:1), and God more often "hears" rather than "sees" humans in crisis (Gen. 3:9; Gen. 18:21; Ex. 3:7).

3. **The ear is the image of *alef*.** Not only is the ear physically reminiscent of the *alef* (a) (see §70/48), the Hebrew word for "ear," *ozen,* begins with an *alef*.

4. ***Alef* is the essence of the Ten Commandments**. The Decalogue begins with an *alef*. This is no coincidence but is indicative of the infinite nature of divine speech. The letter *alef,* as it were, encapsulates the entire Torah in a single letter (compare to *Gen. R.* 1.10).

5. **The ear cannot have enough of hearing.** Unlike the eye, which can be closed off from sensory input, the ear is always open and receiving all sounds within hearing. The Bible, strikingly, gives the ear a status as independent of human will, a true anatomic analogy to divinity that serves the writer of this teaching well. *Alef* signifies infinity, which is realized in embodied form in the human ear/hearing. This teaching is the first in a three-fold interpretation of the word *ozen,* which is made up of three consonants.

THE REVELATION OF THE EAR
(Part 2- *Zayin*) §80-81 (M) / §54-55 (S-A)

And what [is the function] of [the] *zayin* that is written in "ear?"1

As everyone says regarding the Holy One of blessing,

Everything He created in His world,

He gave it its name from its nature,2

As it is written,

For whatever Adam called any living being, the same was its name (Gen. 2:19).

As if to say, its name was its nature.

How do we know its name is its nature?

As it is written, **The name of the righteous is invoked in blessing,**

But the name of the wicked shall rot (Prov. 10:7).

Can his name rot? Rather, his nature is rotten.3

Here too, [the name is] the thing itself.

What is this like? The *shin* [resembles the] root of a tree, 4

But the root of the tree is bent.5

What is the function of the final *shin*?

To teach us that if you take a branch and plant it,

It will take root again.6

[So,] what is the function of *zayin*?

It is the number of the days in the week, teaching you each day has its own power.

And what is its function here?

To teach you just as there is great wisdom, without end, in the ear,

So there is power in all the limbs.7

1. **Zayin that is written in "ear?"** The second consonant in the Hebrew word for ear is *zayin*, the 7th letter of the Hebrew alphabet.

2. **He gave it its name from its nature**. The Hebrew word for ear is not a mere label, ala John Stuart Mills; rather, its name, like all nouns, participates in the essential nature of the thing it signifies. What follows is an interpretive digression to confirm this claim.

3. **Can his name rot?** The logic here extends the argument that the name embodies the thing it describes. When a "name rots," it really means the person possessing that name decays.

4. **Root of a tree.** The Hebrew word for "root," *shoresh*, (XrX), consists of three consonants, *shin-resh-shin*. The three-pronged shape of the *shin* (X) resembles the appearance of a root system.

5. **The root of the tree is bent.** The second consonant, *resh*, (r) is shaped like a bend, just as tree roots are twisted, reinforcing the idea that the noun captures the nature of the object it names.

6. **It will take root again**. The word *shoresh* not only physically resembles an actual root but even hints at its capabilities—the repetition of the letter *shin* as the third consonant of the word *shoresh* reveals that a root can regenerate itself.

7. **So there is power in all the limbs.** So what does the presence of the letter *zayin* in the word *ozen* reveal? While *alef* represents infinity, *zayin* represents the world of boundaries and limitations—seven days that make up time, seven distinct divine powers, seven limbs (See §82/55) that make up the human form. Infinity feeds and fills the finite

Related Biblical Text:

Then YHVH spoke all these words, saying, I am YHVH, your God (Ex. 20:1-2)

things with its power; God is present in all things, in every part of the Cosmos.

GEOFFREY W. DENNIS

THE REVELATION OF THE EAR
(part 3—Nun) §83 (M)/ §56 (S-A)

What is the meaning of the *nun*?
To teach you that the brain
is the principal part of the spinal cord.
It constantly draws from it.1
And if not for the spinal cord,
The brain could not exist.
And without the brain, the body could not exist.
Because all the body needs the brain.
But if the entire body does not endure,
The brain cannot endure.
Thus, the spinal cord inseminates the entire
  body.2
This is the [bent] *nun*.
But here the *nun* is a long *nun*.3
The long *nun* is always at the end of a word
to teach you that the long *nun*
includes the bent and the long.
But the bent *nun* is Foundation,4
To teach you the long nun includes both male and
  female.5

RELATED RABBINIC TEACHING:

The bent Nun and the straight Nun: the faithful [currently] bent [will become] the faithful, straightened (B. Shab. 104a).

1. **It constantly draws from it.** The brain draws from the body through the spinal cord. There are two verbs that appear in different manuscripts: *shoav,* "drawing," and *shoaf,* "inhaling." Regardless, the next lines will illustrate that the writer is describing a reciprocal system, much as we understand the movement of spinal fluid today, but the *Bahir* regards this to be a circulation system of a different order.

2. **The spinal cord inseminates the entire body.** Borrowing from the Pythagoreans and Plato, Jewish physiology believed semen was produced in the brain and flowed to the penis through the spinal cord (*Midrash ha-Gadol*). Thus, the spinal cord [*nun*] connects the brain [*alef*] to the phallus [*zayin*], hence the word. Understand this as a web of interlocking metaphorical associations: the *alef*/brain/God pours life-giving force to the entire *zayin*/body/world through the spine/*nun*/Tree of Life. So the ultimate point of §§79-80 and 83 is that the ear [*ozen*, !za] is a linguistic/visual metonym for the divine economy that is represented in microcosmic fashion by the human body as a whole.

3. **But here is the nun is a long nun.** There are five Hebrew letters that take two different shapes, depending on if they appear at the end of a letter or not (sort of like the English capital letters that begin a sentence); *nun* is one of these. The bent *nun* (n) best illustrates the channel between the brain and phallus, so why is the elongated *nun* (!) here?

4. **The bent *nun* is Foundation.** It sustains the masculine principle operating in God and the cosmos. Taking its cue from the *Bahir,* later Kabbalah designates *Yesod,* "Foundation," the *sefirah* of male generativity.

5. **The long nun includes both male and female**. The letter, with its two forms, hints at the divine syzygy that drives all celestial and terrestrial existence. In the Talmud (*Shab.* 104a), the Sages also argue that all the letters with two forms, if properly understood, contain the processes of redemption. With that in mind, this teaches that the coupling of male and female has salvific power. This extraordinary property of ordinary coitus may also be a cryptic critique of the Christian claim that the messiah must be conceived outside the conventional mechanisms of male and female reproduction.

The Mystical Meanings of the Commandments: The Divine Power of Humanity

THE *SEFER HA-BAHIR* believes deeply in human empowerment, the cosmic potency of human action. Jews today speak of humanity as "God's partners," something the writers of the *Bahir* would likely endorse. But the *Bahir* goes even further than that. It teaches that God depends on us, not just to make our own lives better but to benefit the heavens as well. Sometimes called "theurgy" by scholars, this is the belief that all human actions have the potential to help or hurt the cosmos, God's connection to creation, or even God Himself. It is the *Bahir*'s thesis that it is the duty of human beings, through righteous behavior, to mend the rifts that form between the masculine and feminine sides of God and restore that disrupted divine harmony.

This is a radically different notion of God's relationship to the universe than we find in the rationalist, philosophic traditions of Judaism, which usually insist that God is utterly self-sufficient and needs nothing from creation or its creatures. In more specific terms, The *Bahir* teaches that fulfilling the biblical commandments, whether ethical or ritual, directly contributes to affecting what later Kabbalists will call *tikkun*, cosmic healing.[12] This belief in human theurgic power is another compelling theme in Kabbalah, one that helps inspire the contemporary Jewish idea that we are obligated to perform *tikkun olam*, to "mend the world."

This section will have two types of teachings. The first, such as *Hands to Bless, The Blessing of Descending and Ascending,* and *The Precious Stone and the Sea of Wisdom,* focuses on the cosmic implications of Jewish ritual. The *Bahir* teaches that the ceremonial practices of Judaism are more than mere gestures of divine acknowledgement or folk-ways, but are instead essential to the orderly working of the universe, sort of pass-codes to engage and activate the necessary supernal functions.

The second, typified by *Little Less Than Divine, Torah on High, The Pillar of Righteousness,* and *The Parable of the Beloved Servant,* speaks of how the most virtuous and inspired individuals can achieve a status so exalted that they can merge their will with the will of God. In practice, the *Bahir* insists, this means that not only will such people fully submit to God's wishes, but when humanity needs it to be so, they can bend God's actions to their own wishes.

Texts not included in this section but which have related content: §8(M); §4(S-A); §119(M); §85(S-A); §172(M); §1 16(S-A).

HANDS TO BLESS
§124(M); §87(S-A)

And then Aaron raised his hands to bless the people. (Lev. 9:22)
What is the reason the hands are lifted when they are blessed with this blessing?
Because the hands have ten fingers, hinting toward the ten *Sefirot*
by means of which sky and earth were sealed.1
These parallel the Ten Words.2
In these Ten are included the 613 Commandments.3
[How so?] If you count the letters of the Ten Words,
You will find that there are 613 letters.4
And in them are all 22 letters except *Tet*, which is missing from them.5
What is the reason for this? To teach you that *Tet* is the womb—
And that [letter] is not included among the *sefirah*.6

Related Biblical Teaching:

And you shall join one to the other, making a single stick, so they [the people] shall become unified by your hands (Ezek. 37:17).

1. The hands have ten fingers, hinting toward the ten *Sefirot*. See § 152M. This is based on *Sefer Yetzirah* 1.2, which states the ten fingers correspond to the ten divine potencies.

2. Ten Words. The Ten Commandments, *Ex.* 20:1-14.

3. Included the 613 Commandments. The 10 Commandments are regarded to be a metonym for all the commandments (*Num. R.* 13:16). Though not known to people uninitiated in Judaism, the Talmudic Sages teach that the Torah actually contains 613 divine instructions, 248 positive ("You shall . . . ") and 365 negative ("You shall not . . . "). These numbers are symbolic. The 248 parallel the number of bones in the body, while the 365 invokes the days of the year. Thus the commandments encompass the totality of human experience, both physical and temporal.

4. 613 letters. Actually, the Ten Utterances consist of 620 letters, but an exegetical move (seven are said to refer to the seven days of the week) discounts seven letters, reducing it to the more potent number.

5. Except *Tet*. *Tet* is the only letter that does not appear anywhere in the text of the Ten Commandments (Ex. 20:1-4). Since it is included in the second version of the commandments (Deuteronomy 5:6-18), the *Bahir* assumes this to be a meaningful exception, though the interpretation that follows is exceedingly cryptic. Prior to the *Bahir,* the Talmud taught that since the first tablets were destined to be destroyed, the word *tov*, "good" (which begins with *tet*), was excluded, lest well-being be destroyed in the world along with the stones (*B. B. K.* 54b-55a). That teaching appears to have no obvious bearing here.

6. The *Tet* is the womb. The shape of the letter *Tet* is that of a receptacle open on the top, closed at the bottom.

Why is it excluded from the *Sefirot*? It is an enigma. Perhaps because it takes in blessing from above but does not allow it to flow "downward" (§84M) as the priest does when he transmits God's blessing to the people. Some translate this as "stomach." Since *tet* is the first letter in *t'umah*, "impurity," it means defiling forces are excluded from the *Sefirot*. This last explanation, however, is pure speculation on this author's part.

GEOFFREY W. DENNIS

THE BLESSING OF
ASCENDING AND DESCENDING
§123(M); §87 (S-A)

Rabbi Amorai said, 'Why is it written, 1
**And Aaron lifted his hands for the people to bless
  them, then he descended** (Lev. 9:22)? 2
For didn't he already descend?' 3
Notice [there is a distinction, for] he descended
  from performing the sin offering, the whole
  offering, and the well-being offering, 4
and only now **And Aaron lifted his hands for the
  people.**
Why this 'lifting?' 5
In order that the one who makes the offering[s
  causes them] to be received [in] the innermost
  6
of their source that is in heaven, as we have said.7
For [the sake of] the upper [worlds] 8
to unify them for the unity of them all.
And what of **the people**?
It is written **for the people**, [meaning] for the sake
  of the people.9

RELATED BIBLICAL TEXT:

**YHVH said to Moses, "Tell Aaron and his sons,
'This is how you are to bless the Israelites. Say to
them: 'May YHVH bless you and keep you;
YHVH's Presence shine on you and be gracious to
you; YHVH lift up His Presence toward you and
give you peace'"** (Num. 6:22-26).

1. Other manuscripts credit this teaching to Rabbi Rachumai.

2. **And Aaron lifted his hands.** This gesture is part of the *birkat kohanim,* the "priestly blessing" described in detail in Num. 6:22-26.

3. **For didn't he already descend?** From the altar following the performance of the offerings described in Lev. 9:15-21, which are called **the offering of the people.**

4. **Notice [there is a distinction].** The first descent refers to the physical descent of the priest from the altar platform. The second descent refers to the divine power that the priest draws down upon the people through the ritual of raising his hands. Rabbi Amorai would translate this passage as, **And Aaron lifted his hands for the people to bless them, then *it* descended.**

5. **Why this 'lifting?'** Raising the hands is a mimesis of the ten potencies that link heaven and Earth, a gesture that apparently activates the flow of blessing. This flow moves in both directions, as we shall see.

6. **Received in the innermost.** To be received in the inner sanctum of the Temple on High. The normally prosaic word *lif'nei* (before), in this case, means "innermost," paralleling its use when referring to something being brought into the Holy of Holy, which quotes Ezek. 37:17, **And you shall join one to the other, making a single stick, so they shall become unified by your hand.** By means of the theurgic enactment with the hands, a priest unifies the higher and lower worlds, mending all breaches and divisions.

8. **For [the sake of] the upper [worlds]**. The ritual strengthens the upper realms, allowing them, in turn, to send life-sustaining blessings into the lower realms.

9. **for the people.** The relationship, as mentioned in the previous note, is of reciprocal benefit. The free exchange of theurgic and divine potencies has direct benefits for all humanity. Though the offerings performed in the Temple might seem arcane and lacking in utility, properly performed, they in fact sustain both heaven and Earth.

GEOFFREY W. DENNIS

THE PRECIOUS STONE
AND THE SEA OF WISDOM
§96(M); §65(S-A)

What is the substrate upon which everything is
    engraved?1
And from it the sky is engraved?
It is the Throne of the Holy One of blessing.2
It is the precious stone and the sea of wisdom.3
This parallels the blue of the fringe.4
Rabbi Meir said, **Why is blue chosen from among
    all varieties of colors [for the fringe]?5
Because blue resembles the sea, the sea resembles
    the sky,
and the sky resembles the Throne of Glory.6
As it is written, **They saw the God of Israel and
    under His feet
was the likeness of a brickwork of sapphire, like
    the essence of the sky in clarity (Ex. 24:10).7
It is also written, **As the likeness of a sapphire
    stone
was the semblance of a throne(Ezek. 1:26).8

RELATED BIBLICAL TEXT:

*. . . instruct them to make themselves fringes on
the corners of their garments throughout the
ages; let them attach a cord of blue to the fringe
at each corner (Num. 15:38).*

1. Substrate. Literally *eretz*, "earth." See §22/14.

2. The Throne of the Holy One of blessing. The Throne of Glory (Is. 6:1; Ezek. 1:26) is the archetype of God's power and authority. Sometimes, the throne is treated in very literal fashion; at other times, it is regarded as a metaphor for a more abstract divine quality. In a rabbinic myth, God took a piece of the divine throne and cast it into the primordial abyss. Creation coagulated around it, so it became the *even ha-shetiyah*, "the Stone of the Foundation" of the world (*Tanchuma,* Kedoshim 10). In the *Bahir*, "throne" is another term for the *Sefirot* (§146M, §152M). Thus, all reality is rooted in, and a manifestation of, God's presence and power.

3. **The sea of wisdom.** We have seen elsewhere in *Bahir* (8: S-A4) that "sea" is an esoteric term for Torah.

4. This parallels the blue of the fringe. The Israelites were commanded to wear ritual fringes, including one blue thread, on the corners of their garments (Num. 15:38). This is still observed by the wearing of a tallit, a square ritual prayer shawl, though the blue thread is no longer mandatory because of concerns that we no longer know the proper method for its manufacture.

5. Rabbi Meir Said. B.T. *Men.* 43b.

6. Because blue resembles the sea. The author creates interlacing symbolism and meaning from these mythic and ritual elements. Blue equals "sea," which equals "Torah," which equals "heaven," which represents the Throne of Glory. Therefore, the blue threads of the fringes mystically tie the Jewish people to God's power, because in wearing them, we more closely "resemble" divinity. In other passages, the Throne can signify other divine entities as well (§ 152M).

7. A brickwork of sapphire. The blue pavement under God's feet is the throne, but this image also brings us back to the first line, where the very "earth" under our feet is a divine substance upon which reality is "engraved."

8. As the likeness of a sapphire. There is wordplay at work here. *Sapir* ("sapphire") has the same root sounds as *Sefirot* (the ten divine qualities) and *sipur* ("story"). Thus, the color, almost synesthetically, reveals divine power, order, and speech. The biblical commandment to wear a fringe with a blue thread figuratively "ties" Israel to these entities.

LITTLE LESS THAN DIVINE
§196(M); §136 (S-A)

R. said, "If they so desired,
The righteous could create a world."
What interferes? Their transgressions.
As it is written, [Only] your transgressions
  separate you from your God (Is. 59:2).
If not for your transgressions, there would be no
  distinction
Between you and Him.1
Thus it was that Rava once created a man
That he dispatched to Rav Zeira.
He spoke to it, but it was not [able] to reply.2.
Were it not for your transgressions, it would have
  been able to reply.
And from what would it have replied? For who has
  a soul to insert in it?3
They said to him, is it not written,
So He opened his nostrils and breathed a breath
  of life (Gen. 2:7)?
It is only on account of your transgressions that
  the soul is not pure.4
This is the [only] distinction between you and
  Him.
As it is written, And You have made him little less
  than divine (Ps. 8:6).

RELATED BIBLICAL TEXT:

**This is the *story of humankind*: When God
created the *first* human being, God created that
being in the image of God (Gen. 5:1).**

1. **If not for your transgressions, there would be no distinction.** Humanity could truly be like God, a theme repeated several times in *Gen.* (Chapter 2; 11).

2. **Thus it was that Rava once created a man.** This *ma'aseh,* or tale of the deeds of the Sages, is not original to the *Bahir*. It first appears in the Babylonian Talmud, *Sanh.* 65b, the earliest account of one of Judaism's most enduring myths, creating a golem, an artificial man. In the Talmudic version, Rav Zeira, realizing the person is merely a golem, is offended by the arrogance of the deed and orders the golem to return to dust. Here, the fact that the golem cannot speak is indicative of the limitations of human creativity. If we were free of our sins, we could do all that God does with equal facility.

3. **For who has a soul to insert in it?** The *Bahir* teaches that the power of speech is an attribute of having a soul. This mirrors the teachings of Eleazar of Worms (Rhineland, 13th cent.), who taught speech was the essence of being in the divine image.

4. **That the soul is not pure.** Not pure enough to bestow life to others. In the absence of sin, our breath would be as life-giving as God's. Made in the divine image, every person exists on the very cusp of divinity. Only our inability to consistently make the right choices keeps us from fully realizing that potential.

THE TORAH ON HIGH
§196(M); §137 (S-A)

And You have made him little less than divine (Ps. 8:6).
And what is contained in [the word] "little?"
He has sins but the Holy One of blessing, blessed be,
His name is blessed forever, sins not.1
Though He is triumphant over transgressions,
Does not the *Yetzer haRa* come from Him?2
Rather [it once came] from Him until David slew it.3
Thus it is written, My heart is carved out within me (Ps. 109:22).
So David was able to say, "Since I was able to end it,
No evil lives in me" (Ps. 5:5).
And how was he able to put an end to it?
By his acquisition of knowledge,
from which he did not cease, night and day.
So he was bound to the Holy One of blessing
[by means of] the Torah on High.4
For in every hour that a man is learning Torah for its own sake,5
The Torah on High binds [him] to the Holy One of blessing.

RELATED BIBLICAL TEXT:

In my flesh, I shall see God (Job 19:26).

1. **His name is blessed forever, sins not.** This continues a prior teaching that the only thing that prevents humanity from achieving God-like status is our capacity to sin.

2. **Does not the *Yetzer haRa* come from Him**? In rabbinic psychology, the human personality has two forces pitted against one another: the *Yetzer haTov,* the "Good Impulse," and the *Yetzer haRa,* or "Evil Impulse." These two desires are manifest in people through acts of altruism and selfishness. Only the Evil Impulse is considered here. This rhetorical question is meant as a challenge to the aspiration toward divinity, suggesting that God deliberately installed this flaw in humanity so that we are never intended to achieve this potential. It also raises the ancient philosophical question: how does imperfection flow from a perfect being? This latter question, which could go in several directions, is never explicitly resolved in the teaching.

3. **Rather [it once came] from Him until David slew it.** The response to the question above is this: if we may not aspire, then how is it that certain religious virtuosos can in fact conquer the Evil Impulse within themselves? Here, it is claimed David achieved this feat, as demonstrated by his words in the Psalms. The claim that David was able to do this is novel to the *Bahir*. In the Talmud, it is claimed the *Yetzer haRa* reigned unchecked over humanity until the Sages of the "Great Assembly" subdued it through their virtue (T.B *Yoma* 69b).

4. **The Torah on High**. *Torah shel ma'aleh,* "upper Torah," appears to be something different from the rabbinic concept of *Torah min hashamyim,* "Torah [given] from heaven." The meaning is not clear here but is likely related to the concept of the "soul of the Torah," which appears in the later mystical work, the *Zohar*. In fact, this

passage may have influenced the *Zohar* in this concept. If this is so, then this refers, once again, to the concept of earthly and celestial "correspondence," that everything on Earth (the Temple, man, Torah, justice, etc.) is the mirror refection of more perfect heavenly entities. Thus, studying the earthly Torah "uplinks" one to the heavenly Torah in its perfection, which in turn allows you to participate in God's perfection and so overcome the influence of the Evil Impulse.

5. **Learning Torah for its own sake.** *Torah lishma* is an idiom for studying Torah without utilitarian purpose or ulterior motive. One studies not to master the law or to gain honor, which are desires driven by the *Yetzer,* but only selflessly, out of pure love of God. This attitude is apparently the prerequisite for using the acquisition of knowledge to perfect oneself.

GEOFFREY W. DENNIS

THE PILLAR OF RIGHTEOUSNESS
§102(M); §71 (S-A)

We learned:
There is a single pillar extending from Earth to
  heaven, and its name is Righteous.1
[The pillar] is named after the righteous.2
For if there are righteous people in the world,
  then it is strengthened,
but if there are not, it is weakened.3 It supports
  the world,
as it is written, **And righteousness is the
  foundation** of the world (Prov. 10:25).4
If it weakens, then it cannot sustain the world.
Therefore, even if there is but one righteous
  person in the world,
it is he who supports the world.
Thus it is written, **And a righteous [one] is the
  foundation** of the world (Prov. 10:25).5
You should therefore take My gift offering from
  him first.
Then, "**These** are the gift offerings you should take
  from them"
[meaning] from the rest. What is it?
"Gold, silver, and copper."6

RELATED BIBLICAL TEXT:

*. . . You shall accept gift offerings for Me from
every person whose heart so moves him. And
these are the gift offerings you shall accept from
them: gold, silver, and copper . . . and let them
make Me a sanctuary that I may dwell among
them (Ex. 25:2-3, 8).*

1. Pillar. This refers back to the biblical myth that the earth is supported on pillars above the primordial abyss (I Sam. 2:8; Job 26:11; Ps. 75:3).

2. Is named after the righteous. The notion of the world being sustained by righteous action is based on Gen. 18; Ex. 33:17; *B.* Horayot 12b.

3. It is weakened. The belief that God needs human action to sustain creation, referred to in later Kabbalah as *tsorekha gavoha,* "a need On High," is the lynchpin of mystical teaching about the reasons for the biblical commandments. It is God, as much as we, who benefits when humans act righteously. This need also encompasses those ritual commandments that from our perspective seem to serve no utilitarian purpose. Enacting them strengthens the divine order in ways we cannot fully understand. This will become evident at the end of the passage. There is a phallic connotation of the strong and weak pillar. Whether this double entendre was intended by the author is a matter of debate.

4. The foundation of the world. Elsewhere in *Bahir,* [184] *Yesod,* "foundation," the ninth and masculine *sefirah,* encompasses the "commandments."

5. A righteous one. The word *tzadik* can mean "righteousness" in an abstract sense, as it is translated in line 5, but also, as translated here, a single righteous individual. The prooftext is repeated here to draw attention to that reading in support of the claim that it only takes one person to keep the world going.

6. From him first. The righteous person. Ex. 25:2: "From each *person* whose heart so moves him." This singular individual of heart is the righteous. In verse 3, God's address shifts from third person singular to third

person plural. Why the shift? "them" refers to the rest of us. The list of metals in descending preciousness is taken as a metaphor that emphasizes whose deeds take priority. These gifts build God's *Mishkan,* God's presence on Earth (Ex. 25:8), reinforcing the central argument of the passage.

GEOFFREY W. DENNIS

THE PARABLE OF
THE BELOVED SERVANT
§78(M); §52(S-A)

From whence do we know that Abraham had a
  daughter?
As it is written, **Then Adonai blessed Abraham
  with everything** (Gen. 24:1).1
It is also written, **All is called by My name, I
  created it, I formed it,**
and made it for My Glory (Is. 43:7). 2
Was this blessing his daughter, or perhaps not?
It was his daughter. A parable: To what may this
  be compared?
To a king who had a wholehearted and perfect
  servant.
He tested him with various tests, but he withstood
  them all. 3
The king said, "What can I give this servant, or
  what can I do for him?"
He continued, "Nothing, but to command my elder
  brother to advise him,
watch over him, and honor him."
The servant turned to [the king's] elder brother
  and learned
his qualities. The [elder] brother greatly loved
  him and called him his beloved,
As it is written, **The seed of Abraham, my beloved**
  (Is. 41:8).
He [the older brother] said, "What can I give to
  him, or what can I do for him?
Behold, this beautiful vessel I made, and in it

1. Abraham had a daughter? This refers to a famous Midrash (*Gen. R.* 59:7) that asks, how can Abraham be said to be blessed "with everything" (*ba-kol*) if he doesn't have a daughter? One Sage, with characteristic playfulness toward the language of the Bible, concludes that the verse also means "Then Adonai blessed Abraham with [a daughter named] Kol."

2. Made it for My glory. The author interprets this verse to mean "All" is God's name, the totality of the universe. "Glory" (*Kavod*) is the biblical term for the Divine Presence in creation, i.e., the Shekhinah.

3. Various tests. The Rabbis detect ten trials in the story of Abraham with which God tested him to establish his worthiness (*B. Avot* 5.5; *Pirke de Rabi Eliezer* 26-31).

4. **A parable.** In this enigmatic gender-bending parable, the daughter who is named All (is it Wisdom?) morphs into a male mentor, who is God's gift, teaching Abraham (the servant) everything there is to know about him. S/He is the Divine Presence, while the "treasure of kings" (Ecclesiastes 2:8-10) that the daughter/brother grants Abraham is both worldly success and supreme knowledge of all things. Yet this parable raises as many questions as it answers. If the "king" in the parable is God, why is the feminine aspect of divinity described as God's "elder brother?" Is the "king" actually meant to be the feminine Divine Presence, and the "elder brother" a higher, masculine divine potency? And in the parable, Abraham receives two gifts—the mentoring of the elder brother and the pearls.

5. Worthy in his place. This alludes to the episode in *Gen.* 18 where Abraham questions God's plans for the city of Sodom. The rabbis teach that the exchange between God and Abraham shows us the status of the righteous is such that they can query the divine mind and even change that

beautiful pearls without rival, treasures of kings.4
I will give it to him and he will be worthy in his
   place."5
This is the meaning of **Then the Lord blessed
   Abraham** with everything.

RELATED BIBLICAL TEXT:

***Then Adonai** went when He finished addressing
Abraham; Abraham returned to his place (**Gen.
18:33**).*

mind. The episode ends with the words: "Then Abraham returned to his place." Abraham was capable of rising above "his place," excelling past normal human limitations with regards to the divine. Yet even when not in direct communion with God, Abraham occupied an honored and exalted place in creation.

THE SOUL AND DEATH:
THE DEATH OF DEATH

ONE OF THE most durable and, for modern Jews, appealing teachings of the Kabbalah is the belief in the transmigration (*gilgul*) of souls. *Sefer ha-Bahir* is the wellspring of that teaching. Until recently, many Jews were unaware that there is a belief in reincarnation at all in Judaism, this esoteric belief being overshadowed by the older, exoteric belief in resurrection, which has been enshrined in Jewish liturgy. Nevertheless, Jewish mystics claim it is an eternal feature of the cosmic order. Critical scholars see reincarnation as a historical development, while traditionalists insist it has been present in Jewish tradition from the beginning. Intriguingly, there develops a complex interplay that developed between the teaching of reincarnation and the much older Jewish doctrine that the human spirit is polypsychic; the soul is compounded of three (or here, five) distinct aspects. Usefully, these distinctive "soul sparks" allow later Kabbalists to reconcile differing Jewish teachings about the fate of the soul; the different elements undergo different journeys and processes of rectification.

As often happens, the first time someone decides to writes about a subject, it is in order to criticize it. On this matter, we know that as early as the 10th Century, Jewish rationalist philosopher Sa'adia Gaon ridiculed the idea of metempsychosis, of the transfer of the soul from body to body, but Sa'adia does not cite the document or group that inspired his ridicule, leading to much speculation about other Jewish groups of the time.[13] In the past, scholars have linked Jewish belief in reincarnation to the rise of Karaism, a movement that competed with the rabbinic tradition that defines Judaism as we know it today. But the question of who or what Sa'adia was reacting to has been given a new and tantalizing possible explanation now that a good case has been made for parts of the *Bahir* having their origins in 10th Century Mesopotamia.[14] Was Sa'adia responding specifically to teachings now found in the *Bahir*, or the people who composed its earliest version? Impossible to know, given our current level of knowledge, but this suggests that belief in transmigration of the soul may in fact be one of the earlier controversies to divide Jewish rationalist from Jewish mystic. Whatever the context, reincarnation appears late in the history of Jewish ideas, but it first gets a *positive* presentation here. Even within the teachings that follow, they, too, suggest that the concept of souls transmigrating from body to body was both novel and unfamiliar to most Jews.

What we do know is what followed after the *Bahir*, that reincarnation became integral to later works of Kabbalah. It became so widely accepted, in fact, that in the 17th Century, the rabbi and public intellectual Manasseh ben Israel would tell a Christian correspondent that reincarnation was no less than a dogma that all Jews needed to acclaim.

That ascendancy was short-lived. Reincarnation faded from popular consciousness, along with many other metaphysical beliefs, with the rise of the Jewish enlightenment. Only traditional communities with strong continuing ties to kabbalistic literature, such as Hasidism, continue to maintain a familiarity with this conception of the Hereafter.

The essential teachings concerning reincarnation in the *Bahir* are outlined in the homilies that follow: *The Golden Power of the Five Souls*; *The Parable of the*

Servants' Garments, which introduces the concept; *The Parable of the Vineyard,* which addresses a little of the metaphysics but also integrates earlier tradition into the schema of transmigration; and *Redemption Through Body and Soul,* which reveals the messianic dimension of metempsychosis.

Texts not included in this section but which have related content: §40-41(M); §20(S-A)

THE GOLDEN POWER
OF THE FIVE SOULS
§53(M); 34 (S-A)

Why is gold called *zahav*?1
Because it incorporates three qualities.
Zachar, it is the masculine. This is the *Zayin*.2
Nashamah, the soul; that is the *hay*,
For the five names of the soul: 3
Ruach, *Chayya*, *Yechuda*, *Nefesh*, and *Neshamah*.
And what is the function of the *hay*?
It is the seat for the *Zayin*.4
As it is written,
For an exalted one is over an exalted one,
  guarding (Eccl. 5:7).5
The *bet* is its foundation,
As it is said,
When God began to create the heaven and the
  earth (Gen. 1:1).6

RELATED BIBLICAL TEXT:

My beloved is radiant and ruddy, pre-eminent among ten thousand. His head is pure gold (Song of Songs 5:10-11)

1. **Why is gold called *zahav*?** This continues an earlier discussion, in §48, of the verse, **Mine is the sliver, Mine is the gold** (Hag. 2:8). "Gold," in the earlier discussion, is an encoded term for "God's right hand," divine might and justice. Later, Kabbalah will designate this attribute as the sefirah *Gevurah*. This teaching argues the nature of this power is revealed in its very name, which is actually an acronym.

2. ***Zachar*, it is the masculine.** The root of this word means both "male" and "memory." The second sentence is far from subtle. A *Zayin* is the shape of a phallus. In fact, the word *zayin* is an idiom for a penis.

3. **The five names of the soul.** In Gematria, *hay* has the numeric value of 5. Here, the argument moves from seeing the word as a pure acronym to arguing the letter is a numeric *remez,* a "hint" of the hidden reality. The idea that the soul has five *names* come from *Gen. R.* 14:11. Later mysticism revises this into a belief that the human soul is polypsychic, it has five distinct sub-souls.

4. ***Hay* . . . is the seat for the *Zayin*.** This is a remarkably blunt and rather bawdy interpretation of the shape of the letters. The letter *hay,* with its three closed sides and opening on the bottom, is seen as a stylized vagina.

5. **For an exalted one is over an exalted one, guarding.** Position the *zayin* beneath the *hay,* and the result is orthographic—and mystical—coitus.

6. **When God began to create.** As we have learned in section 2, the *bet* is a starting point of divine emanation, the introduction of duality that yields positive existence. The *bet* unleashes the forces of generativity that populate the cosmos with all beings and entities. This binary force

is the *dynamis* of creation, God's power, eventually to be labeled *Gevurah*. Desire is the flywheel of creation, the essence of the human soul, and, contrary to the attitude of some other philosophies and religions, directed properly, is the source of all good.

GEOFFREY W. DENNIS

THE PARABLE OF
THE SERVANTS' GARMENTS
§121-122(M); §86 (S-A)

What is [the meaning of] **Generation to generation**
(Ps. 164:10)?

Rabbi Papias said, **A generation goes and a
generation comes** . . . (Eccl. 1:4).

Rabbi Akiba said, **a generation comes** . . . that
already came.1

A parable. To what may this be compared? To a
king who had servants

and as much as he could he dressed them in
garments of silk and embroidery.

The grain spoiled.2

So he pushed them from him and sent them away.

He took their garments, so they left them.3

[The king] took the garments and cleaned them
well until not a stain remained.

He placed them near Him for an appointed time.

He acquired other servants, and dressed them in
the same garments.

Though he did not know if they were any good
[either],4

they were worthy of garments that already existed

and had been worn by others before them. . . . **but
the earth stands forever.5**

And this is as what is written [elsewhere], **the
dust returns to the earth as it was,6**

but the spirit returns to God who gave it (Eccl.
12:6).7

1. That already came. In a previous incarnation, referring to transmigration of souls from generation to generation of bodies. The parable that follows is based on several that appear in the B.T. *Shab.* 23a, 152b, revised to reflect a belief in reincarnation.

2. The grain spoiled. They both failed in their obligations and, at the same, time soiled the king's garments. The individual who transgresses soils God's gift, his soul, with sin.

3. He took their garments, so they left them. Their bodies passed away. This sly parable defies our expectations by making the garment (the soul) not the servant (the body/our current incarnation) the central concern of the allegory.

4. **He did not know.** A curious statement. Is the writer suggesting God cannot know the decisions a person will make in the future? If so, this is a rejection of the classic theistic claim that God is omniscient, a central pillar of scholastic philosophy. This, then, anticipates the similar claim made by the Jewish philosopher Gersonides by several centuries.

5. **But the earth stands forever.** At first glance, this proof-text seems to serve no function. It may be that this is intended as an oblique refutation of the idea of bodily resurrection held by the earlier sages, as if to say, "the body will never return, but . . . " and then the next verse follows.

6. **The dust.** The body.

7. **The spirit returns to God.** To transmigrate as God sees fit.

Related Biblical Text:

Truly, God does all these things two or three times to a man: To return his soul from the grave that he may bask in the light of the living (Job 33:29-30).

GEOFFREY W. DENNIS

THE PARABLE OF THE VINEYARD
§195(M); §135 (S-A)

Why does the wicked man prosper and the
   righteous suffer?
[R. Rachumai replied] Because this righteous man
   was once a wicked man in the past,
and is now being punished.
[They asked him:] But is a man punished for the
   sins of his youth?
Did not Rabbi Shimon say that the heavenly court
   only punishes a man
for [the sins he commits from the time he is]
   twenty years old?1
[R. Rachumai] replied: I do not speak of the
   [same] life;
I speak of the fact that he was already there in the
   past.
His colleagues said to him: How long will you
   speak enigmatically?
He said to them: Go and see! A parable:
What may the matter be compared to? It is like a
   man who planted a vineyard in his garden,2
and he hoped it would grow grapes, but it grew
   wild grapes.
He saw that his planting did not succeed,
so he cut down the vineyard, tore it out, and
   cleaned the good grapes from the wild ones,
and planted it a second time.
When he saw that that did not succeed, he tore it
   down and planted after he had cleaned it.
When he saw that [the third planting] was not
   successful, he tore it out and [re]planted it.

1. Twenty years old? B. *Sanhedrin* 89a; *Num. R.* 18:3.

2. A man who planted a vineyard. This parable breaks with several conventions. It only states the premise obliquely before the parable begins, though this can be seen elsewhere; it breaks with the stereotypical introductory formula; and it makes the protagonist a "man" rather than the more conventional "king." Nonetheless, the protagonist is still a figure for God.

3. Until the thousandth generation. The parable ends without a *nimshal*, though the point seems to be clear: the souls of those who have lived before and died because of their sins continue to be reincarnated until their souls have atoned for the crimes of their former lives. This can continue indefinitely.

4. 974 generation were missing. This complicates the seemingly straightforward point, for the number 974 alludes to a Talmudic tradition that God created multiple worlds before ours and destroyed them because of their radical imperfection. In God's compassion, however, the souls of those worlds, some 1000 generations, God has preserved to undergo metempsychosis in this incarnation of the cosmos. The reduction from 1000 to 974 has to do with the 26 generations between Adam and Noah having already undergone this process (*B. Chag.* 13b; *Shab.* 88b; *Mid. Teh.* 90:13)

5. Blessed One arose and planted them in every generation. All the souls of the dead from God's failed prior worlds continue to be reincarnated, to this day, until their souls are fully rectified. This seems to narrow the application of reincarnation. The righteous who suffer are those who possess souls (or parts of souls) that predate the origins of this iteration of the cosmos.

And how many times? Until the thousandth
  generation,3
as it is written, **The matter He gave to a
  thousandth generation** (Ps. 105:8).
And that is to say: 974 generation were missing,4
so the Holy One of blessing arose and planted
  them in every generation.5

RELATED BIBLICAL TEXT:

*For the vineyard of YHVH of Hosts is the house of
Israel, and the men of Judah are the garden in
which he delights (Is. 5:7).*

REDEMPTION THROUGH BODY AND SOUL
§184(M); § 126 (S-A)

The Treasuries of the Souls are in its [Yesod]
  hands.1
And when Israel is good,
The [new] souls in the Treasuries
merit to go forth and to enter this world.2
But if it is not good,
They do not go forth
So it was, the Sages taught,
The Messiah will not come
until all the souls in the guf are done (Talmud,
  Yev. 62a,b).3
What does it mean, all the souls in the guf?
The human body.4
And [when] the [last] new [souls] are permitted
  to go forth,
only then is the Messiah permitted to be born.
How so? Because he will come out [new], like the
  other [new souls]. 5

RELATED BIBLICAL TEXT:

***Why are you downcast, O my soul? And why are
you disquieted within me? My hope is in God,
because I will praise him once again, since his
presence saves me and he is my God (Ps. 43:5).***

1. **In its [Yesod] hands**. Based on the teaching that precedes this one, "it" is the *sefirah* of Yesod/Righteousness. Not only is this divine potency the source of all life in the universe, its moral power makes it the point from which cosmic redemption will also overtake the world (See §102/§71).

2. **The [new] souls**. This teaching further explores the metaphysics of reincarnation. When the people Israel, who are central to the salvific drama of all humanity, fail to fulfill their redemptive role in the world, their souls must transmigrate, and no new souls from the great Treasuries of Souls may begin their journey. Only when they act properly are the already existing souls able to complete their soul tasks and reunite with the Godhead, making room, as it were, for the remaining soul in the Treasuries.

3. **The Guf.** *Guf* is the Hebrew word for "body." There are two primary interpretations of this: First, this refers to the body of every human, which is polypsychic; it contains three (or more) souls (See: §53/§34**).** Less likely, but still plausible, this refers to the supernal body of Adam Kadmon, the macro-cosmic, primordial first man who appears frequently in rabbinic teachings (B. *Nid.* 13b; *B.B.* 58b; *Gen. R.* 8.1, 34.14; *PdRK* 4:4, 12:1, *Lev. R.* 14.1, 20.2). In later centuries, mystics such as Chayyim Vital would teach that all human souls are in fact fragments of the *guf* of the Adam Kadmon, which functions as the Treasuries of Souls, or the World Soul (*Etz Chayyim*: Derush Igulim ve-Yosher 4:28a:1-15). This commentary is going to assume the first interpretation.

4. **The human body.** Until every soul spark has left the Treasury of Souls and completed its cycle through human hosts.

5. **He will come out [new]**. Though the belief that the *idea* of the eschatological Messiah preexists the world can be found in Jewish sources (*Gen. R.* 1.1), his soul has not yet entered the world. It is easy to take this as a veiled refutation of the Christian doctrine of the first and second comings, or even the Shia Muslim doctrine of the Hidden Imam. But if it is, it is not very pointed. More likely, this is a teaching that incorporates older traditions about the advent of the Messiah with this novel concept of reincarnation. The compelling new reason offered for why the Messiah has not yet come is because he will be a new soul of sufficient righteousness, he will not require cycles of transmigration, and the souls of those already living have not yet advanced themselves enough to receive him.

The End of the Matter
The Promise

The Reconciler of Opposites
§59(M); 40(S-A)

Why is heaven called *shamayim*?
Teaching that the Holy One of blessing blended fire
    and water,
and combined this to that,
making from them the first of His word.1
As it is written,
The first of Your word is truth (Ps. 119:160).2
And it was [also] written,
Shamayim, [meaning] 'there is water' [and] 'fire
    and water.'3
And he said, thus **The One who makes peace in His
    high places** (Job 25:2).
May He also place peace and love among us.4

Related Biblical Text:

*For the mountains may depart and the hills be
removed, but my steadfast love shall not depart
from you, and my covenant of peace shall not be
removed," says YHVH, who has compassion on
you. (Is. 54:10).*

1. **The first of His word.** Torah. The Torah is compared to both fire and water (Jer. 23:29; Isaiah 55:1) and is given through fire and water (*Num. R.* 1.7).

2. **Your word is truth.** The "word of God" is a common metonym for Torah.

3. **There is water [and] fire and water.** This seems to be a non sequitur in translations, but in Hebrew is a pair of wordplays. By means of *tzeruf,* letter re-ordering, the word *shamayim* renders the words *yesh mayim* ("There is water"), or *aish* and *mayim* ("fire" and "water"). These interpretations are very old (B. *Chag.* 12b; *Gen. R.* 4.7).

4. **May He also place peace and love among us**. A coda to the Book of Brilliance, as well as to the mystical quest itself: the promise of an end to the burden of all dualities. God, who brings symmetry and transformation in the highest dimensions of being, similarly will reconcile the irreconcilable in the lower worlds. If we would but listen.

GLOSSARY

Alef—First letter of the Hebrew alphabet.

Bet—Second letter of the Hebrew alphabet.

Cholam—the diacritical mark that represents the "long O" vowel sound.

Dalet—Fourth letter of the Hebrew alphabet.

Ein Sof—"Without End/Boundless One." God as Deus *absconditus,* unknown and unknowable.

Gimel—Third letter of the Hebrew alphabet.

Habakkuk—A minor prophet of the Hebrew Bible. *Sefer ha-Bahir* devotes a significant amount of effort interpreting a small number of verses from his book.

Hay—Fifth letter of the Hebrew alphabet.

Heder—"Chamber/room." This word can also mean "secret," or the female reproductive organs. The *Bahir* frequently uses this word in double and triple entendres.

Hechal—"Palace." In ancient Jewish mysticism, the seven *hechalot* and their angelic denizens are a mythic embodiment of the divine emanations. This term overlaps with *Merkavah* and *Pleroma*.

Kavod—"Glory." The biblical term for the Divine Presence.

Mashal—"Parable."

Merkavah—"Chariot." The divine chariot and its features—beasts, radiances, wheels, and attendant angels—is another shorthand term for the divine order.

Midrash—"Inquiry." The distinctive rabbinic method of Bible interpretation that makes extensive use of intertextuality, philology, and linguistic anomalies in the text.

Nimshal—"Moral/analogy." The explanation of a parable.

Nun—Fourteenth letter of the Hebrew alphabet. Orthographically, it has two shapes, the *nun* and *nun sofit*.

Ofan—a multi-eyed "wheel" angel, as described in Ezekiel, chapter 1. There, such angels are the wheels of the divine chariot. Elsewhere in Jewish tradition, they cycle between heaven and Earth.

Polysemy—The capacity of a word to have many meanings. Many interpretations in the *Bahir* depend on the polysemy of a Hebrew word.

Pleroma—"Fullness." A Greek term for all things divine; the celestial order. See **Merkavah** and **Hechal.**

Rabbi Amorai—This mysterious sage appears in no other rabbinic sources, leading to speculation this is a pseudonym for Rabbi Nechunya.

Rabbi Nechunya ben haKanah—1-2nd Century Talmudic sage. He also appears in several early mystical texts. As the teacher of another rabbi closely tied to the mystical tradition, Rabbi Ishmael, he came to be widely identified as the author of the *Bahir* (see the introduction).

Rabbi Rachumai—1st Century Talmudic sage. A minor figure in the Talmud, he features prominently in the *Bahir*.

Sefer Yetzirah—"Book of Formation." A brief mystical treatise on the Hebrew alphabet and numerology. It contains the first references to the *Sefirot.*

Sefirot—"Numerals." Ten divine qualities that emanate from God's essence.

Shekhinah—"In-dwelling." The rabbinic term for the Divine Presence, usually characterized as feminine.

Syzygy—"Yoked [pair]." The belief that divinity manifests itself in the world through the duality of masculine and feminine attributes.

Tefillin—"Phylacteries." Ritual leather boxes containing biblical verses worn by Jews on their left arm and forehead during daytime prayers.

Ten Utterances—The ten speech-acts in *Gen.* by which God created the world.

Ten Words—*Aseret Dibrot.* In English, we say, the Ten Commandments.

Torah—"Teaching/Instruction." This word can mean one of two things. "The Torah" is a closed set; it refers to the Five Books of Moses: *Gen., Ex.* , Leviticus, Numbers, and Deuteronomy. "Torah," on the other hand, is open-ended, referring to the totality of Jewish teachings, practices, and beliefs.

Yetzer haRa—"The evil inclination/desire." Often contrasted with the Yetzer haTov, the "good inclination," it refers to the internal human impulse to do what is selfish, evil, or contrary to the teachings of Torah. At times in Jewish literature, it is reified as a demon-like force or entity.

YHVH—The Tetragrammaton, or four-letter (*yud-hay-vav-hay*) name of God, which Jews have largely ceased to pronounce out loud since early post-biblical times. Appearing over a thousand times in the Hebrew Bible, it is the subject of extensive and diverse interpretations by both Jews and Christians; linguistics, philosophers, mystics, and magicians.

Zayin—The seventh letter of the Hebrew alphabet.

TABLE OF BIBLICAL CITATIONS

(Underlined citations appear in the text of the *Bahir*; all others appear as or part of the annotations).

Genesis

Proverbs

Job

Ecclesiastes

Song of Songs

INDEX

A

Aaron, 186, 190, 191
Abraham, 7, 22, 51, 64-67, 122-122, 208-211
Abrams, Daniel, 7, 9, 255
Adam, 65, 67, 131, 133, 164, 174, 255
Adam Kadmon, 164, 229
Alef, 40, 42-45, 46-47,51, 59, 75, 93, 96-97, 157, 172-173, 175, 179, 237
Amirin, 111
Amorai, 92, 190, 191, 238
Androgyny, 130, 139
Angels, 12, 14, 33, 77, 109, 110, 123, 136-137, 164, 167, 238
Asah, 131
Axis Mundi, 70, 75, 99, 101

B

Bara, 133
Beginning, 41, 42, 50-53, 72-73, 81, 97, 133, 144, 213
Brishti, 50,51, 53,
Bet, 53, 54-55, 161, 216, 217, 237
Binah, 43, 57, 116, 139
Birds, 79, 130, 133, 148
Blessing, 29, 30, 41, 46, 51-53, 64, 76-77, 82-83, 98-99, 102, 105, 106, 130, 155, 164, 166, 172, 174, 184, 186, 189, 190-191, 194-195, 200, 208, 226, 234
Blue, 194-197

N
Nefesh, 216
Nehunya ben ha-Qanah, 8
Neshamah, 59, 216
Nimshal, 12, 77, 93, 103, 141, 143, 145, 149, 159, 225, 238
Notarikon, 11
Nun, 58-59, 178-181, 238

O
Olam katan, 164

P
Pagan, 16
Parable, 11, 12, 28, 29, 31, 50, 53, 76, 77, 88, 89, 92, 93, 102, 103, 118, 119, 136, 137, 140, 141, 144, 145, 147, 148, 149, 152, 153, 156, 157, 159, 160, 161, 184, 208, 209, 214, 215, 220, 221, 224, 225, 237, 238
Paradox, 23, 24, 25
Plato, 10, 12, 75, 163, 179
Pleroma, 13, 14, 33, 73, 77, 87, 109, 137, 139, 145, 155, 169, 237, 238
Polysemy, 11, 59, 238
Princess, 11-12, 128

R
Rabbinic literature, 10, 12, 13, 29, 131
Rachumai, Rabbi, 32-33, 36, 76, 191, 224, 238
Rav Zeira, 198, 199
Rava, 198, 199
Reincarnation, 9, 61, 213-214, 221, 225, 229, 231
Resh, 40, 107, 175
Right, 14, 115, 116, 118-121, 153, 163, 166, 217
Righteous, the, 82-83, 174, 198, 204-205, 209, 224, 225
Ruach, 45, 216

ENDNOTES

1) Gershom Scholem, *On the Kabbalah and its Symbolism,* (New York: Schocken, 1969), 90.

2) Daniel Abrams, *The Book Bahir: An Edition Based on the Earliest Manuscripts* [Heb.] (Los Angeles: Cherub Press, 1994), iv.

3) Abraham J. Heschel, *Man is not Alone: A Philosophy of Religion* Philadelphia, Jewish Publication Society, 1951), 129.

4) Daniel Abrams, *"Bahir," Encyclopedia Judaica* (New York: Gale Publishing, 2008).

5) Moshe Idel, *Kabbalah and Eros* (New Haven: Yale University Press 2005),49-52.

6) See the discussions by Gershom Scholem, *Origins of Kabbalah,* 62-63; 162, 167, and by Elliot Wolfson, "The Tree that is All," *Along the Path: Studies in Kabbalistic Myth, Symbolism, and Hermeneutics.* (New York: SUNY Press, 1995).

7) Eitan Fishbane, "The Speech of Being, the Voice of God: Phonetic Mysticism in the Kabbalah of Asher Ben David and his Contemporaries," in *The Jewish Quarterly Review,* Vol. 98, No. 4 (Fall 2008) 492.

8) Simo Parpola, "The Assyrian Tree of Life: Tracing the Origins of Jewish Monotheism and Greek Philosophy," *Journal of Near Eastern Studies,* Vol. 52, No. 3 (Jul., 1993), pp. 161-208.

9) Joseph Dan, *The Early Kabbalah*, (Mahwah: Paulist Press, 1986).

10) Moshe Weinfeld, "Feminine Features in the Imagery of the God of Israel: The Sacred Marriage and the Sacred Tree," *Vetus Testamentum,* 46:1 (1996), 515-529.

11) As argued by Dan Abrams, "The Condensation of the Symbol Shekhinah in the Manuscripts of the Book *Bahir*" *Kabbalah* 16 (2007), 10. Some would disagree with this, claiming the ideology of the *Shekhinah* is already fully developed in the *Bahir*. See Ronit Meroz, "The Middle Eastern Origins of Kabbalah," in *The Journal for the Study of Sephardic and Mizrachi Jewry,* 1:1 Summer 2007, 53.

12) Daniel Matt, "The Mystic and the Mizvot," in *Jewish Spirituality: From the Bible through the Middle Ages.* Edited by Arthur Green (New York: Crossroads Press, 1994), 367-404.

13) Sa'adia ibn Yusuf Gaon, *The Book of Doctrines and Beliefs* (New Haven: Yale University Press) Vol. 1, 259.

14) Meroz, Ronit, 2007.

About the Author

Geoffrey Dennis is rabbi of Congregation Kol Ami and Chief Rabbi of Denton County, TX. He is an instructor of Bible, Rabbinic Literature, and Kabbalah at the University of North Texas.

He is the author of this book, the *Encyclopedia of Jewish Myth, Magic, and Mysticism* (2015), and has published articles, book chapters, essays, and academic encyclopedia entries.

www.ingramcontent.com/pod-product-compliance
Lightning Source LLC
Chambersburg PA
CBHW030902060726
47591CB00005B/1383